WHAT OTHERS ARE SAYING ABOUT THIS BOOK

No matter how big your organisation, if you are involved in fundraising, you need to read this book from one of Australia's most thoughtful and progressive fundraising professionals. Having worked with Pamela in a few different roles, I have always valued her approach to fundraising. Her high degree of innovation, governance and commercial acumen has helped many organisations leverage their fundraising strategy to ensure sustainability.

Sarah Franklyn, Chair, Seddon Community Bank
(Inner West Community Enterprises)

Pamela joined Zoos Victoria in 2010 and lead the Foundation for five years. In this time, she developed our philanthropy approach and strategy, and she delivered the Safe Haven campaign, which raised over $20 million for improved facilities, better animal welfare outcomes and a greater contribution to fighting extinction. Pamela leads with a combination of head and heart. By articulating a clear strategy and plan, she enabled the Foundation Board and Zoo Executives to support her work and to actively contribute. Pamela is fierce in delivering targets and understanding the financial impacts of philanthropy work.

Dr Jenny Gray, CEO, Zoos Victoria

Pamela is an excellent community director who engages business and community leaders to strengthen their social enterprise.

Andy Moutray-Read, CEO Inner West Community Enterprises

I have enjoyed volunteering with Pamela at community activities. She is a great asset to our community by sharing her skills and knowledge of the not-for-profit sector.

Dr Marilyn Olliff, 2019 Hobsons Bay Citizen of the Year, Chair, Hobsons Bay Wetlands Centre

I have no doubt you will benefit from Pamela's fantastic new book. I've known Pamela for almost 20 years and have loved working with her in two major fundraising roles: Plan International and Bush Heritage Australia. Pamela is a visionary with years of fundraising and marketing experience who excites others, achieves results and brings you on the journey with her.

Bev McLennan, Liaison, Melbourne Deaf & Hard of Hearing Lions Club

In this book, Pamela shares insights and wisdom gained from more than 20 years as a fundraising professional. I have seen her in action – she's an extremely effective fundraiser and has built and managed multi-million dollar campaigns. She's an inspirational leader and is highly creative in her approach to finding new ways of bringing in income for not-for-profits, large and small.

Charlotte Francis, Grants Specialist and Writer, Charlottefrancis.com

Pamela is a very effective fundraiser who achieves success with enthusiasm, strength of purpose and grace. I have known Pamela in staff fundraising roles and as a consultant providing strategy to fundraising leaders and to charity boards. Her accomplishments have been achieved across all charitable sectors and all fundraising types – these are rare achievements and position Pamela well to write The Fundraiser's Handbook.

Dr Daniel McDiarmid, Director, AskRight

The Fundraiser's Handbook

Contact pamela@fundraisershandbook.com for
free fundraising resources

The Fundraiser's Handbook

Create a winning fundraising strategy
and raise more money

Global Edition

Pamela Sutton-Legaud MBA CFRE

First published in 2024
Global edition

ISBN: 978-0-6453777-2-9 (pbk) eISBN: 978-0-6453777-3-6 (ebook)

A catalogue record for this book is available from the National Library of Australia

Edited by Joanna Yardley

Typeset by BookPOD

WHO THIS BOOK IS FOR

In the first edition of The Fundraiser's Handbook, I included insights specific to the Australian fundraising market. This updated global edition will help fundraisers wherever they are in the world to achieve their fundraising goals.

This book is primarily for fundraisers of non-profit organisations who want to raise more money for their cause. Raising funds for your organisation is a challenge. This book will guide you through the process by using a powerful yet simple template that will get you on your way to raising more money.

You may already raise funds through a variety of channels such as direct mail, email and face to face, and from several sources, for example, individual donors, foundations or corporations. However, I am sure (without looking at the specifics of your organisation) that whether you are paid to fundraise, are a volunteer, have years of experience or have never attempted to fundraise before, you could be conducting your fundraising more efficiently and effectively and, therefore, could be raising more money.

Fundraising is a learned skill. I will teach you the processes, practices, systems and structures to help you raise more money than you thought possible. Here is my first piece of advice: start today.

PREFACE

Thank you for choosing this book to help you deliver great fundraising results for your organisation. I will show you many tools that have helped me raise more than $150 million for non-profit organisations.

For more than 30 years, I continued to fundraise as a senior executive working in the education, conservation and international aid sectors with Oxfam Australia and Plan International. I returned to the conservation sector with Bush Heritage Australia and Zoos Victoria to help protect Australia's threatened species.

More recently, and for the past six years, I have worked as a strategic fundraising consultant providing advice to many non-profit and for-purpose organisations including schools, community groups, social ventures and charities. I helped these organisations create strategies to generate more money so they could become more financially sustainable.

Every fundraiser has *that* moment when they ask themselves, *Where do I start?* I've certainly had many of those moments in my fundraising career. During those times, I have reached for the one proven tool that has helped me to overcome uncertainty—a written fundraising strategy.

If the idea of writing a fundraising strategy scares you, please take a breath and know that this book will help to eliminate that fear. By taking a step-by-step approach and using a proven templated structure, I will show you how to prepare, write, execute and measure the results of your strategy so that every time you set out to fundraise, you will achieve better, more predictable results.

Whether you are a seasoned fundraiser or just beginning your journey or whether you are a paid staff member, a director or an occasional volunteer, this book will help guide your organisation to deliver on its goals and give your donors wonderful experiences.

So much in life requires just a bit of confidence. I will help you to build confidence in yourself and your organisation. You have a cause that deserves to be supported, and you **can** raise more money than you have in the past. I will help you bring your cause to your donors' attention and motivate them to support you.

This book will help you clarify your goals, write a strategy that will keep your organisation afloat and prepare you for future challenging times. You will learn:

- key ways to raise more money
- how to use your current resources
- how to utilise and leverage assets at your disposal
- where to find new donors and how to keep them.

ACKNOWLEDGEMENTS

Thank you to everyone who has helped bring this book to life (past and current colleagues and clients included). I have learned so much from all of you.

I dedicate this book to my mother, Liz, my husband Christophe, my aunt Marie and my sisters, Carol and Sandra.

ABOUT THE AUTHOR

I was born in London, England, after my parents moved there from Dublin, Ireland. While I'll always be a Londoner, Melbourne, Australia, has been my home for more than 30 years, and it is a place I love.

After a career with the international brand and direct marketing agency Ogilvy & Mather Direct in London, as well as Lintas and Leo Burnett in Melbourne, I refocused my career to align with my values and became a permanent part of the non-profit sector.

I started my career in the community sector as an enthusiastic volunteer in the mid-90s when I began my own non-profit organisation to protect wild tigers from poachers. I was motivated to action by a poster created by The Body Shop when it was run by Anita Roddick. The poster was protesting that there were only 5,000 wild tigers left. I couldn't believe this statistic—I had always loved these beautiful animals and the thought that they were being slaughtered for the traditional medicine market made me incredibly sad and angry. That was the push that got me into the charity sector.

I soon realised that to be an effective charity and make a difference, I needed resources. I decided to learn more about creating change. Since that humble start, I have created and led strategies that have raised more than $150 million for non-profit and for-purpose organisations in Australia including Oxfam Australia, Plan International, Bush Heritage Australia, Zoos Victoria and many client organisations.

Since 2016, as a strategic fundraising consultant, I have provided fundraising advice and helped many organisations achieve their fundraising goals. From 2017 to 2021, I was Principal Consultant with AskRIGHT—an international fundraising and strategic planning consultancy where I worked with charities and non-profit organisations of all kinds. I have served on non-profit boards including Trust for Nature, Connecting Home (a service for the Stolen Generations), Seddon Community Bank, Hobsons Bay Community Fund and BirdLife Australia.

I am dedicated to helping all non-profit organisations effectively and efficiently deliver on their missions. I have an MBA and am a fellow of Fundraising Institute Australia. I am a Certified Fund Raising Executive (CFRE) and an Australian CFRE Ambassador. For my work with Plan International and the 2006 Melbourne Commonwealth Games I was recognised as a Victorian Telstra Businesswoman of the Year.

I live in Williamstown, Victoria, with my French husband who supported and encouraged me to write this book, and our cat, Beau, who knows when to provide a cat hug.

All this shows that you never know where life will take you.

Working with Pamela

If you would like direct assistance or advice on your fundraising goals, please email me at pamela@fundraisershandbook.com or visit my website www.fundraisershandbook.com.

CONTENTS

STAGE 4: EVALUATE YOUR FUNDRAISING STRATEGY

HOW THIS BOOK WORKS

This book is structured in two parts:

Part 1 sets the scene for fundraising principles and the landscape in which you will fundraise. We will discuss why you need a fundraising strategy. Here you will learn about the principles of asking for money and get an introduction into the different types of donors and why people donate.

Part 2 introduces you to the fundraising strategy template, which is broken into four stages. I will guide you through the steps in each stage so you can create your own fundraising strategy. I have drawn on my experience as a strategic fundraising professional to create an effective 4-stage fundraising strategy that you will prepare, write, implement and evaluate.

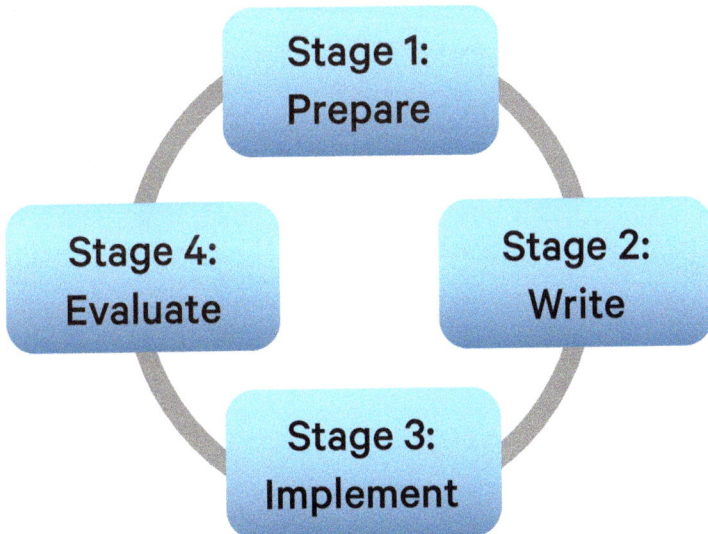

Stage 1: Prepare

Stage 2: Write

Stage 3: Implement

Stage 4: Evaluate

Stage 1: PREPARE Your Fundraising Strategy

This is where you'll compile the information you need to prepare your fundraising strategy. You'll identify the information you'll need to collect, for example, what your organisation is all about, why you are fundraising (your cause), what you need the funds for, who will benefit and, importantly, why anyone should support your cause. You'll review what level of resources you have available to invest in your strategy in terms of people, tools, time and money.

We'll go through these in detail so you can determine the most important information needed to build your strategy.

Stage 2: WRITE your fundraising strategy

In Stage 2 you will clarify your strategic approach. This includes developing your unique selling proposition (USP). The preparation in Stage 1 will give you the basis to decide on your goals and objectives using SMART goals. Your strategic approach and your goals will help you define your expenditure and income budgets. Yes, you do need budgets. We will consider how to identify, select and qualify potential donors and why each type of donor requires a different approach. We will discuss how fundraising and marketing are integrated and how AIDA (Attention, Interest, Desire, Action) is used to attract donors. You will read about the fundraising funnel and the Donor Ladder of Loyalty. All of this will put you in the best position to go for your goals.

Stage 3: IMPLEMENT your fundraising strategy

Once you've done the hard work of writing your strategic approach, you will implement it. Stage 3 is all about **how** you will deliver your strategy and achieve your goals. You will clarify who your target audience is and which fundraising channels you can use to reach it. You will learn how to write a brief to internal and external suppliers, how to create an implementation calendar, how to test elements of your strategy before full rollout and how to manage donor data and privacy. We'll consider how to implement annual fundraising appeals, a direct mail campaign, a corporate sponsorship plan, an events plan, a gifts in wills program and a major gifts plan. Here you can utilise the Value/Effort matrix to determine whether the time / effort you are putting into your strategy is giving you the value you want.

Stage 4: EVALUATE your fundraising strategy

It's satisfying to see the results of all your efforts and to use that information to improve your next fundraising strategy. What would you do differently next time? In order to measure this, you need to create Key Performance Indicators (KPIs) and consider any risks that may impact the results you are trying to achieve. This is ultimately where we compare the experience you have been through with the results you achieved and consider how you can do it better in the future. Finally, we will look at how to develop a risk management plan to develop contingencies in case the unexpected happens.

By the time you have finished, you will have a written document that will provide the direction you need to take decisive action and raise more money.

PART 1

SETTING THE SCENE

'Go confidently in the direction of your dreams! Live the life you've imagined.'

—Henry David Thoreau

WHY YOU NEED A FUNDRAISING STRATEGY

Your fundraising strategy is the map that will take you from where you are now to where you want to go. Like any map, it will describe the terrain you will cross, the challenges you will face, the opportunities you will discover and the final destination. It will help you determine what routes to follow, how long the journey will take and who will travel with you. It will capture the cost and the return.

If your immediate response is *I have a strategy; it's in my head,* then you do *not* have a strategy at all. At the heart of this book is the belief that a well-written, well-executed strategy will outperform wishful thinking—or a lack of any strategy—any day of the week.

A written strategy will help you do the following:

a. **Get your thoughts and ideas on paper.** The very act of writing down your goals can help you clarify where you want to go (or not go, as the case may be). Writing down your strategy is the best way of keeping you and others on track.

b. **Create a document you can share with others.** In most organisations, you will need to share your strategy with others in order to gain approval, support, funding, resources, etc. This is only possible if your strategy is written down. Sharing your fundraising strategy means you can get feedback on your ideas before you fully commit to them. You can clarify areas of confusion or vagueness, and you can work with your team to help it become a joint strategy.

c. **Create a record of your goals and objectives.** It is easy to lose track of where you are heading. You can forget your primary purpose if you don't have a written plan of attack. It is a good idea to create measurable financial and strategic goals. (See SMART goals and objectives.)

FUNDRAISING FUNDAMENTALS

Fundraising is a means of helping your organisation to deliver on its goals by engaging with like-minded individuals who will financially support your cause.

Here are ten fundraising principles that underpin the thinking of this book:

1. *Have a written strategy*

I think I've made this point but just in case you missed it, the most useful tool to help you to raise more money is to create a written fundraising strategy. Having a fundraising strategy is important for small and large organisations, for those that have been operating for many years and for those that would like to expand their services or raise more money from individual donors.

2. *Be consistent with your mission*

Like all activities conducted within your organisation, fundraising activities should be consistent with your organisation's mission, vision and values. Your fundraising should be mission-driven. This means not accepting funds for projects that do not match your vision. It also means conducting fundraising activities that enhance your vision and mission.

3. *Generate a return on investment (ROI)*

The primary goal of fundraising is to deliver a positive financial return for your organisation. This assists the organisation to deliver on its mission and achieve its goals. While individual activities may deliver varying degrees of success and take more or less time to deliver a return, overall, your fundraising strategy should forecast a positive financial result.

4. Conduct fundraising activities in good faith and for the benefit of your constituency or community

Acting in good faith means that your fundraisers are using the information provided to them to deliver the best fundraising results for your organisation. Their intention is to deliver positive outcomes with the organisation front of mind in all activities. No individual should benefit from fundraising activities—the aim is to put the organisation and its mission first.

5. Be transparent

At all times, the leaders within your organisation should be able to use systems and processes to see how much has been spent and how much has been raised. Good fundraising strategies need to be transparent to leaders with regular reporting and benchmarking against goals. The methods and results of your fundraising should be transparent to your donors.

6. Co-operate

The best results come from thorough co-operation between fundraisers and other teams, donors and key stakeholders. When the entire organisation is working together to achieve its funding goals, great things are possible and will happen.

7. *Integrate fundraising with your marketing strategy*

Strategic Planning - How it's connected

*Government Grants can sit outside the fundraising strategy but it should acknowledge government funding objectives and opportunities for synergies.

Fundraising is a discipline that sits within a marketing framework. If it stands alone, away from the other operational areas of an organisation, it is destined to deliver less than if it were an integral part of your organisational strategy and structure.

As the fundraising department cannot deliver on its KPIs in isolation, the fundraising strategy should form a part of your organisation's strategy—the two should work in collaboration. The main aim of a fundraising strategy is to help provide the funds that will enable the organisation to deliver its primary purpose.

8. *Commit to a high level of executive engagement*

An integrated strategy requires a high level of executive engagement—not just from the marketing or finance departments. All managers across all departments should understand and support the KPIs of the fundraising strategy and have a specific part to play in its success. Who will read your strategy? And more importantly, who has the right to approve or invest in your strategy? Be clear, from the beginning, who you need to consult.

9. Follow an ethical code of conduct

Professional fundraisers follow the guidance of their industry peak bodies and their country's ethical code of conduct and legal framework. In Australia, fundraisers commit to the Fundraising Institute Australia (FIA) Code of Conduct. Many fundraisers from around the world are endorsed as a Certified Fundraising Executive (CFRE) with CFRE.org.

10. Ask for money

While some donors will give without being asked, most will not. Donors must be cultivated. This means someone needs to identify, cultivate and 'ask' a potential donor to give and steward them to give again.

These fundamentals for best practice fundraising are emphasised throughout this book to ensure greater success.

OVERCOMING THE FEAR OF ASKING FOR MONEY

There is an old expression that comes from sales gurus, 'Nothing happens until somebody makes a sale'. There is a similar one for fundraising, 'Nothing happens until someone makes 'the ask'', so let's deal with the elephant in the room early.

Many people fear making 'the ask' more than any other aspect of fundraising, particularly, when they think about asking for a donation face to face. They fear it to such an extent that they will not even talk to their colleagues or raise the subject of fundraising at a board or leadership meeting.

In most cases, this fear is unfounded. This is not the primary support we want from our leaders. We do not *always* expect our directors, managers or volunteers to actually ask donors for donations. What we're looking for is their personal commitment and their positive engagement with the organisation's fundraising strategies to help those who are strong in making 'the ask' have more success.

As a fundraiser, you will need to ask for money and you'll do it in a range of ways including face to face, online and via mail and telephone. Let's consider why people may donate.

WHY PEOPLE DONATE

It may surprise you to know that the main reason people donate is because they were asked. According to an academic literature review of more than 500 charitable giving articles conducted by Rene Bekkers and Pamala Wiepking, there are eight drivers for why people donate to a charity:[3]

1. Awareness of need.
2. Solicitation.
3. Costs benefits.
4. Altruism.
5. Reputation.
6. Psychological benefits.
7. Values.
8. Efficacy.

Awareness of need and solicitation (asking) are the most important. Awareness means the donor becomes aware of a need that your organisation will meet. This is the number one reason. If they are not aware of the need, they are unlikely to give. Solicitation is when somebody asks them to donate. Having become aware of the need, someone asks them to make a gift. These two drivers go the farthest to underline the reason why fundraising and fundraisers are essential to helping non-profit organisations deliver value to their constituencies. A donor needs to know about your cause **and** be asked to donate.

Donors may, of their own volition, get around to donating to you because they support the work you do. But be assured, the most effective way to get someone to donate to your cause is to ask them to give.

MAKING 'THE ASK'

When you are considering making 'the ask', there are five things you can do to improve your chances of receiving a 'yes' to your question—particularly when you ask in person.

1.   *Be prepared*

Before you consider asking for a donation—no matter the size—you should be prepared. This means having a good understanding of your prospect's level of interest in your organisation, their capacity to donate a certain amount of money, and their existing connection to your work and organisation.

2.   *Be polite*

You can compare asking for a donation with marriage courtship. Usually, you would ask someone out to dinner once or twice (at least) before proposing marriage. Therefore, the first time you meet someone is not the time to ask for a significant donation. Take the time to get to know your potential donor before you make 'the ask'. By the time you're ready to make a request for a donation, you should be fairly certain that you will get some kind of positive response.

3. Be organised

When asked the question, 'Who should ask for the donation?' most people think the answer is 'the fundraiser'. In fact, the right person to make 'the ask' is the person who is most likely to get 'yes' as the answer. Large donors in particular like to be asked by those whom they consider to be peers. So if your chairperson knows a prospective donor well, it may be helpful to have them in the room when the request for a donation is made—even if they don't actually make 'the ask'.

And what if there is no one else but you to make 'the ask'? If this is the case, make sure you have done everything you can to understand your potential donor's interest and connection to the cause. Know your donor, understand their needs and interests, and know what you want to ask them.

4. Be specific

It is important to be specific about what you want. Vagueness is not helpful in fundraising. If you want $10,000 to help fund a scholarship program for young aboriginal women in the Kimberley, then say exactly that. Do not amble into 'the ask' with 'Please could you support our scholarship program?' In this case, you are likely to either get nothing or get a lower donation than you had hoped. As mentioned before, by the time you ask for your donation, you should have established that your prospective donor is interested in supporting *your* organisation to help young aboriginal women and that they have the capacity to give $10,000. If you are unsure whether this is the case, go back a step. This will help you know how much to ask for and for which project.

5. Be brave

In more than 20 years as a fundraiser, I have never had a donor get angry with me because I asked for a donation. Mostly they would say 'not now' and be happy to be asked again in the future. Something amazing happens, however, when the donor says, 'Yes, I would love to make that gift'. It is transformational for both the organisation and the donor because you have both achieved something: as the fundraiser, you are a step closer to helping your organisation deliver on its mission, and the donor has made a step towards fulfilling their own philanthropic goals.

Philanthropy is something important for both the organisation and the donor. It is worth a moment of anticipation and a little fear to reach this milestone, so prepare, be brave and take a chance.

A BACKGROUND TO GIVING

WHAT DONORS LOOK LIKE

Here is a list of donor types and the ways they can donate.

1. *Individual donors*

These donors are individual people who give once, occasionally or often using a range of methods:

a. **One-off donations:** These are donations that are given once and after which you will need to ask again, such as when someone donates to your end-of-year appeal.

b. **Regular donations:** These are donations that are committed to in advance and given on a fixed periodic basis such as monthly, quarterly or annually. Regular donations are often made automatically by direct debit from a bank account or a credit card. They offer a forecastable source of revenue when you attract them in volume.

c. **Workplace giving:** Employees in companies sometimes set up regular donations to be paid to a charity from their gross salaries. These are called workplace giving donations.

d. **Major donations:** These individual donations are larger than your usual donations. You can decide what you classify as a 'major donation' (possibly $5,000 or above). This definition can change as your donations grow and as the size of individual donations increases.

e. **Bequests, legacies, gifts in wills:** Whichever term you choose to use, bequests, legacies or gifts in wills are donations left to your organisation in the final will of the donor. You only receive the funds after the donor has died. It can take 4–5 years from the time you set up and start to implement a bequest program before a bequest arrives. According to the Pareto Benchmarking Study, in 2018, $258 million was received from bequests by Australian charities, the largest figure ever with an average bequest of $65,000.[4]

2. Companies

Sponsorship: Sponsorship funds come from a company that wants to leverage your brand (and your good work) to help it sell its own products or services or to enhance its own brand. Most corporations have a corporate social responsibility (CSR) strategy, which relates to their corporate strategy and outlines the types of causes or organisations they want to support. They will give funds to organisations whose causes make them look good in the eyes of consumers.

Corporate donations: Some companies will give philanthropic donations perhaps via their company foundation through grant programs, via fundraising activities undertaken by their staff or by a Workplace Giving scheme where employees donate a specific amount from their gross pay to a charity. Even in this case, most of the donations are from individuals within the company. Most philanthropy comes from individual donors. My experience is that there is almost no corporate philanthropy; it is primarily sponsorship.

3. *Trusts and foundations*

Trusts and Foundations provide grants. These are entities created for the purpose of donating funds to non-profit organisations. For larger and more established trusts and foundations, you will need to make a formal application. For smaller grants, you will need to identify the trustees and find a way to connect with them in order to make a submission for a grant. Grants can be for one year or multiple years and can be tied to specific deliverables or to fund the running of your operation. They are a good source of major donations, i.e. donations above $5,000.

4. *Government*

Governments will also provide grants and have formal application processes and strict selection criteria. In this book, we will not look at government funding.

TYPES OF PHILANTHROPIC FUNDING

It is often challenging to find donors who will support particular projects or programs. This brings us to the two main types of funding: tied and untied. The most useful form of funding is untied funding, which you can spend as you choose on your main priorities. The other form is tied funding.

UNTIED FUNDS

Untied, unrestricted or flexible funds can be used for any purpose your organisation sees fit. These are the most useful funds you can attract as you can use them to implement your programs and pay for staff or other operational requirements for which it is hard to attract tied philanthropic funding.

To a certain extent you can decide how you treat the funds you receive. You can allocate these funds to whatever priority you see fit. Just make sure that what you have told your donors when you asked for the donation matches where you will spend it.

TIED FUNDING

Tied funding is sometimes called fixed or restricted funding. It is provided for the purpose of delivering a specific project, service or other deliverable that the donor or grantor has chosen to support. You must use the funds for the purpose for which they were given. If the deliverable does not proceed, you must either offer to return the funds or ask the donor if you can apply the funds to another project.

The types of funding you can receive or request depends to some extent on the legal structure of your organisation. This requirement will impact what your fundraising strategy looks like.

THE DONOR CULTIVATION JOURNEY

So let's talk about donors and how to encourage them to donate. As you prepare your strategy, you will also consider the donor cultivation journey. This is where you'll take the donor on a journey to identify, qualify and ask as they learn more about your work and vision and join with you to achieve it.

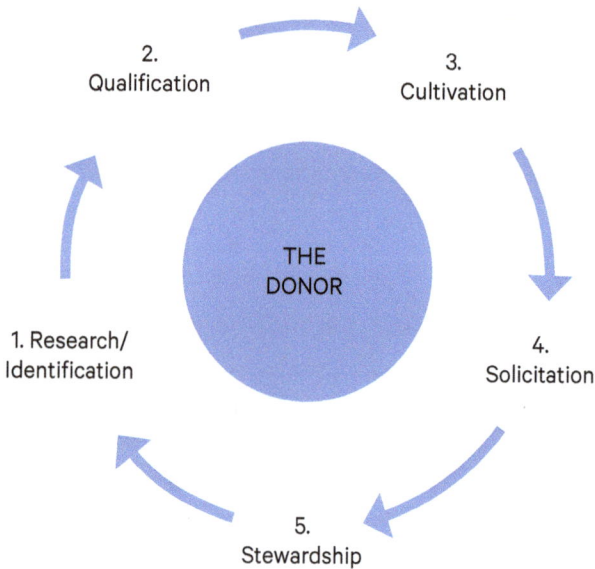

This is the donor cultivation journey. It is a continuous journey. The donor is always at the centre. Some donors will drop out along the way so we must identify new donors to take their place with research.

Research and identification

This is where you determine who you want to target. This is why we include research and donor identification early in our plan in Stage 1.

Qualification

Not all donors are equal. When you qualify a donor, it means you have done sufficient research to understand whether they have a link, inclined or capacity (L.I.C.) to give to your organisation. This is an important step for larger donors. Even if you are trying to attract smaller donors, you can try to better understand their interests and motivations before you ask for a gift. This is qualification.

Cultivation

Before you can ask a donor for a gift, your relationship with them needs to be cultivated. That means helping them to understand and be interested in the work for which you need funds. You will not always want to jump right in and ask for a donation cold. You may like to warm the relationship up first. You do this by developing donor plans, deciding on fundraising channels plans, creating engagement materials and hosting activities (events).

Solicitation

This is the action you take to get a donation from a donor or multiple donors. You may ask one-on-one in a face-to-face meeting or via direct mail. However you do it, you want to be as prepared as possible to make 'the ask'. We will deal with this in Stage 3 when we cover implementation.

Stewardship

This is the stage after you have received your donations. Now is not the time to stop talking with your donors. You want to build the relationship and keep them involved in your cause and vision. There are actions you will take to provide feedback and continue your contact. We will go over this in Stage 4: Evaluate your fundraising strategy.

So now you have some background on the environment in which you are working. You can now work through each stage of the four stages of your fundraising strategy using the fundraising strategy template to guide you.

PART 2

THE 4-STAGE FUNDRAISING STRATEGY

Stage 1: Prepare your fundraising strategy

Stage 2: Write your fundraising strategy

Stage 3: Implement your fundraising strategy

Stage 4: Evaluate your fundraising strategy

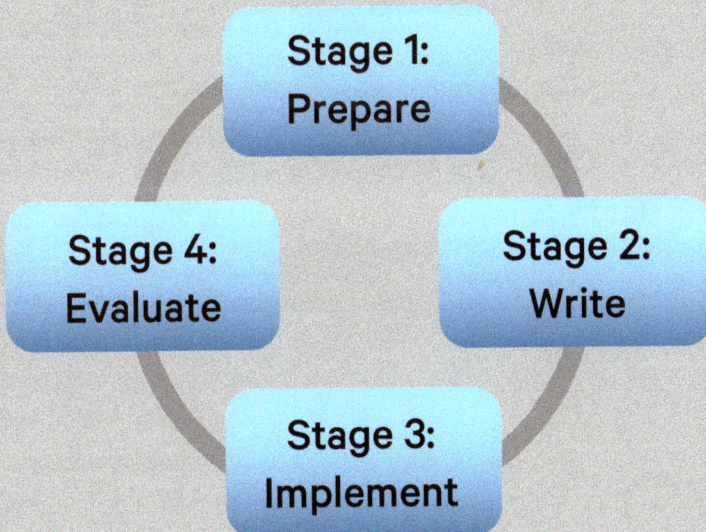

Stage 1: Prepare

Stage 2: Write

Stage 3: Implement

Stage 4: Evaluate

4-STAGE FUNDRAISING STRATEGY

To produce an effective fundraising strategy, we will follow four stages:

- Stage 1: Prepare your fundraising strategy
- Stage 2: Write your fundraising strategy
- Stage 3: Implement your fundraising strategy
- Stage 4: Evaluate your fundraising strategy

At the beginning of each stage, you will see the specific steps you need to follow to complete that section. In this way, by the time you have worked your way through the four stages, you will have a thorough and effective strategy.

HOW TO GET STARTED

The first step is to create a folder on your computer and call it '[Your organisation's name] Fundraising Strategy'.

Open a Word document or an Excel spreadsheet—wherever you prefer to capture the information you locate. Name it 'Fundraising Strategy Template'.

Create a table with four columns and use the headings in the template below. In that template, you'll also see the four stages with a set of steps to consider for each stage. There is a column for you to mark off your progress as you collect the information and save it in your 'strategy folder'.

There. You have created your (albeit blank) fundraising strategy document. This is the document where you will capture information about the resources you'll need in order to achieve your fundraising goals and determine the structure of your fundraising strategy.

So let's get started with Stage 1: Prepare your fundraising strategy.

4-STAGE FUNDRAISING STRATEGY		
STEP	**DESCRIPTION**	**YOUR PROGRESS**
Stage 1: Prepare your fundraising strategy		
1	Current situation 1.1 Vision and mission 1.2 Key stakeholders 1.3 Key deadlines	
2	Related policies and procedures	
3	Situation analysis 3.1 Where you are now 3.2 Why are you raising money? What needs will you meet? 3.3 What projects need funding? 3.4 What's your Case for Support? 3.5 Who are you and why should you be doing this work? 3.6 Who will implement the work on the ground? 3.7 How much will it cost to implement the work? 3.8 Why should anyone support your cause?	
4	Resources 4.1 People (paid staff and volunteers) 4.2 Tools 4.3 Time 4.4 Money	
5	Analysing donors and prospects 5.1 Existing donors and prospects 5.2 Developing demographic donor profiles 5.3 Profiling and qualifying prospects 5.4 Donor acquisition	
Stage 2: Write your fundraising strategy		
6	Strategic approach and competitive advantage	

4-STAGE FUNDRAISING STRATEGY		
STEP	**DESCRIPTION**	**YOUR PROGRESS**
7	Your unique selling proposition (USP)	
8	SMART (Specific, Measurable, Actionable, Realistic, Timebound) goals and objectives	
9	Determine your target audience/s 9.1 Turning suspects into advocates: the Ladder of Loyalty 9.2 The donor pyramid 9.3 Donor retention and growth	
10	Fundraising income and expenditure budget 10.1 Budget by type of donor 10.2 Budget by marketing channel 10.3 Determine your net return	
Stage 3: Implement your fundraising strategy		
11	Attract donors' attention: the AIDA Principle	
12	Determine marketing and fundraising channels 12.1 Direct response marketing vs mass marketing 12.2 Direct marketing appeals or campaign structure 12.3 Digital fundraising 12.4 Channel integration	
13	The Value/Effort matrix	
14	Create targeted fundraising plans 14.1 Structured campaigns and fundraising appeals 14.2 Developing a bequests, gifts in wills or legacies plan 14.3 Grants (applications to trusts and foundations) 14.4 Corporate sponsorship 14.5 Events 14.6 Major gift and capital fundraising campaigns	

4-STAGE FUNDRAISING STRATEGY		
STEP	**DESCRIPTION**	**YOUR PROGRESS**
15	Doing it all 15.1 Using outside suppliers 15.2 A campaign brief 15.3 The implementation calendar 15.4 Test. Test. Test.	
16	Caring for donor data 16.1 Donor financial data 16.2 Prospect data 16.3 Donor privacy and data protection	
Stage 4: Evaluate your fundraising strategy		
17	Measures of success 17.1 KPI dashboard 17.2 Return on investment (ROI) 17.3 Donor lifetime value	
18	Donor stewardship	
19	Ethics and accountability 19.1 Donor Charter and Donor Bill of Rights	
20	Contingency planning and risk management	

Stage 1

Prepare your fundraising strategy

'I keep six honest serving-men (they taught me all I knew). Their names are What and Why and When and How and Where and Who.'

—Rudyard Kipling, *The Elephant's Child*

PREPARE YOUR FUNDRAISING STRATEGY

In Stage 1, you will bring together all the information you need to inform your fundraising strategy. Here you will compile the background and organisational review to capture all the background information about why you are fundraising. You will work through the first five steps on your fundraising strategy:

4-STAGE FUNDRAISING STRATEGY		
STEP	DESCRIPTION	YOUR PROGRESS
Stage 1: Prepare your fundraising strategy		
1	Current situation 1.1 Vision and mission 1.2 Key stakeholders 1.3 Key deadlines	
2	Related policies and procedures	
3	Situation analysis 3.1 Where you are now 3.2 Why are you raising money? What needs will you meet? 3.3 What projects need funding? 3.4 What's your Case for Support? 3.5 Who are you and why should you be doing this work? 3.6 Who will implement the work on the ground? 3.7 How much will it cost to implement the work? 3.8 Why should anyone support your cause?	
4	Resources 4.1 People (paid staff and volunteers) 4.2 Tools 4.3 Time 4.4 Money	

4-STAGE FUNDRAISING STRATEGY		
STEP	**DESCRIPTION**	**YOUR PROGRESS**
5	Analysing donors and prospects 5.1 Existing donors and prospects 5.2 Developing demographic donor profiles 5.3 Profiling and qualifying prospects 5.4 Donor acquisition	

Step 1: Current situation

1.1 Vision and mission

To kick off your strategy, write down where you are now. Capture the name of your organisation, its purpose and mission, and any key information about your current situation. What is happening with your organisation? What is the current status of fundraising? Everything you do in your fundraising strategy will be driven by your mission and vision, so it is important to capture it clearly at the start of your document.

1.2 Key stakeholders

Capture the key stakeholders in your document so you are clear, from the beginning, who you need to consult. Who will read your strategy? And more importantly, who has the right to approve or invest in your strategy? Who will make decisions or help you make decisions about your fundraising strategy?

Stakeholders can be internal, for example, your team, your manager, the CEO, the board and council. Stakeholders can also be external, for example, suppliers, project partners, key donors and corporate partners.

1.3 Key deadlines

If you are writing this strategy, someone else will want to read it. You may therefore need to comply with key dates like a forthcoming board meeting where all strategy documents will need to be presented. There could also be a date when all budgets need to be approved or sighted by the finance team. It is important to understand and capture this early in the process so you don't get to the point of implementation before finding out you can't get the budget you need or vital human resources have been allocated elsewhere.

If you are unsure, ask your manager or board member about who needs to be involved to help make your plan a reality. There may be multiple people who will need to sign off on your strategy or perhaps it's just you. It's best to be sure and document this early.

Step 2: Related policies and procedures

Are there any policies by which this fundraising strategy is governed? If you don't have these policies in place, keep going. It is always helpful for an organisation to have a policy framework but you can work on that later. Focus on your fundraising. In the meantime, consider whether you need to review and comply with any of the following:

- Corporate sponsorship policy: Are there specific organisations or types of organisations from which you will not accept funds or collaborate, for example, alcohol, mining or cigarette companies?

- Gift receipt policy: Are there certain gifts you will not accept, for example, the proceeds of gaming or gambling?

- Bequest policy: How will you manage any bequests? Will they go to particular projects or be treated as 'untied' funds?

- Purchasing policy: If you work for a large organisation, there may be rules about which suppliers you use.

- Delegation policy: If you manage a budget, you will likely have delegated maximum amounts that you can spend. If you are unsure, ask what your financial maximum spend is without seeking permission. This is really useful information as you don't want a campaign held up because no one can agree on how much you can spend.

Step 3: Situation analysis

3.1 Where you are now

A situation analysis spells out where you are now. This is helpful for those who may read your strategy without knowing its context. It provides the reasons for the strategy and the challenges it hopes to address. It will help you in months to come when you look back on the strategy. In addition, by setting the scene in this way, you will help connect your current situation with your goals.

If you are updating an existing fundraising strategy, you can refer to previous documents or research you have used to get this far. You will likely want to improve on previous results; therefore, you can state those results and the conditions under which you are creating the new strategy.

This analysis doesn't need to be long and you can add to it as more information becomes available. For now, we are just setting the scene for what comes next.

3.2 Why are you raising money? What needs will you meet?

These are the most fundamental questions you can ask yourself and your organisation. They go to the heart of why anyone should donate to you. It is worth remembering that people donate because an organisation *meets* needs and not because it *has* needs. It is not enough that your organisation needs help. You need to show them that their donation will help solve problems that the donor cares about.

Right now, you want to capture your cause as simply as possible. Here are a few examples:

- We want to build a school in Africa for children affected by HIV and AIDS.
- We want to extend our school's sports grounds.
- We want to build a community swimming pool.
- We want to help children with impaired vision to see.

Your fundraising cause should be as clear as possible. If you know why you are fundraising, you can communicate more effectively with donors and motivate them to fund your vision.

3.3 What projects need funding?

To attract money from donors, you need to know what issues and needs you will address with their donations. For donors to give, they need to care about the projects you will complete and believe that you are the right organisation to complete them. The more specific you can be here, the better you will be at communicating your needs to potential donors.

Be donor-centric. Consider what your donor cares about—not just about what you want and need. Take the time to understand the project(s) for which you want to raise funds. This may seem obvious but it is worth delving into. If you want funds for a building, where will the building be located? How much will it cost to build? Do you already have the land or do you need to raise funds to buy that too? What is the purpose of the building and who will benefit from it? Or, if you want to raise funds

3.8 Why should anyone support your cause?

This is an interesting question. If you are thinking that it's obvious because your cause is very important ... sorry, but it's not obvious at all. You need to spell out *why* your cause is important. What needs are you meeting?

Here are some things to consider when you are thinking about your *why*:

- **Competition**: There are likely several organisations that do the same or similar work to you. How are you different? Why should a donor support you and not them?

- **Outcomes**: Can you show that you have or can deliver real outcomes for your constituency or beneficiaries? Outcomes are not the same as outputs. For example, an output is a plan and an outcome is the result of implementing the plan. You want to show that the object of your fundraising will be improved in some way by raising the money.

- **Meaning**: What does your cause mean to your donors? Can they relate to the work you do and the things you want to achieve? Can you connect the focus of your work with your donors' values?

- **Value**: Can your donors see that you provide great value? How efficient is your organisation at delivering on its promises? Can you do it cheaper or quicker than others? Can you do it with less staff or less money? Can you do it with lower operating costs?

- **Innovation**: Are you doing things differently to others? Have you developed new technology or research that will deliver results in a new way? Can you help your donors understand why this innovation is important?

This information will inform your strategy and give you the content you need to create your fundraising assets.

Step 4: Resources

Your team may be made up of a few skilled team members, some volunteers (always have volunteers) and you. Figure out the resources you have and the resources you may need. The four important resources we will consider are **people** (paid staff and volunteers), **tools**, **time** and **money**.

4.1 People (paid staff and volunteers)

It is possible to raise funds on your own and some very passionate people do this, but one person cannot sustain the level of energy required to fundraise single-handedly for very long. Plus, if you are the only person raising money, you will not deliver the organisation's full fundraising potential nor be able to service all of your donors, and you will eventually burn out and move on. You'll be far more effective by fundraising as part of a team, whether that team consists of a few part-time volunteers or an experienced leadership group.

Know your team, and work with people who understand that fundraising is a team sport.

Clarify who is on your team and the skills you need covered. Who will help you implement your strategy? Whether you have a paid team or a team of dedicated volunteers, it is important that everyone knows that they will be involved in the implementation of this strategy.

It helps to consider what skills and experience will be most useful. For example, if you are hoping to implement most of your fundraising using online, digital or eMarketing techniques, it will be helpful to have someone on your team who understands those areas; otherwise, you will need to be a fast learner and be willing to make some basic mistakes before you get a handle on these channels. If you know you won't get the funds to pay for the resources you need, consider whether you can get some of the skills for free or if you need to change your strategy.

While there are many fundraising tasks that will need attention, consider some of the following categories:

- **Research**: Conducting desktop research on current and prospective donors; liaising with external research companies; investigating grant opportunities.
- **Data**: Collecting, compiling and analysing data in spreadsheets; entering data into a customer relationship management (CRM) system, database or spreadsheet; tracking donor engagement activities.
- **Donors**: Calling or meeting with donors to discuss priority projects; sending out grant applications or proposals; following up donor meetings; calling or writing thank-you letters; sending out receipts.
- **Finance**: Entering donations into CRMs, finance systems or spreadsheets; creating donor receipts; tracking donations received; creating reports on donations received and funds spent.
- **Events**: Creating and sending out invitations; booking venues and suppliers; creating giveaway bags; organising seating arrangements; booking entertainment; running raffles and charity auctions.
- **Social media**: Creating accounts; monitoring user questions and queries; releasing information and sharing photographs.
- **IT and website**: Creating website; management of account including passwords; management of security; content

updates; integration with other systems, for example, finance or donor CRM.

These categories represent some of the basic requirements to implement your strategy. You may not have one person for each category. It may all be down to you and a few volunteers. But it is a good idea to articulate what may need to be done and consider who is going to do the work.

Volunteers

If you can't afford paid staff, think about volunteer time. When we think of volunteers, we often imagine people 'stuffing envelopes'. But you can attract skilled volunteers—people who understand direct marketing, social media marketing and website building. Seek out reliable, skilled and enthusiastic people who will help you deliver your strategy. Even a few dedicated hours from someone with knowledge and experience can make a difference to your results. You can search on Seek.com for volunteers or reach out to your network / friends / family who may have the skills and time to help you.

If it is not already the case, provide everyone who is working with you with a job description and ensure fundraising is stipulated as an activity for which they have some responsibility. This is important, otherwise resources that you thought you could rely on can just say, 'It's not my job'. This also applies to volunteers. Ensure each volunteer has a written job description that outlines the work they will do during their volunteering time. This helps achieve at least two things: it helps people know what their work involves and it helps attract people who want to do that type of work.

One area you can look to for support is your finance or accounts team. A long time ago, I discovered that the finance team or accounts department is the fundraiser's best friend. The 'finance department' in your organisation may only be one person working part time or maybe there is a team of people. Either way, the finance department understands numbers. They understand Excel. They understand budgets.

In my experience, finance teams are often neglected. All they do is count the money, right? Wrong. These amazing people can help you understand how the money works and how best to present it in a way for you and everyone else to understand what you will deliver and how much it will cost to deliver it. Take one (or all of them) out to lunch or for a coffee and ask them for help with your expenditure budgets and forecasting your fundraising income. Budgets are the backbone of business cases. A budget will help you get funds from your executive team to invest in your fundraising strategy.

You may also need them to help you run reports on what money has come in and what money has been spent.

You need to know your way around budgets and money. So befriend your accountant or bookkeeper and ask for their help. They are a part of your team.

4.2 Tools

You will also need non-human resources such as databases, websites and other tools that will make the job of fundraising easier and more efficient. Consider some of the following when you are documenting what is available to you:

Website: In this digital age, you will need an effective interface between you and prospective donors and this will take the form of a functioning website. Many donors will find out about you via your website, and as we've learnt, knowing about your cause and being asked to give are the two main reasons why donors donate. Every non-profit organisation should have a website and it should have at least one 'donate' button.

CRM / database: In order to effectively capture, manage and manipulate donor data, you will need a CRM system or a donor database. In the event that your organisation cannot afford to invest in a CRM, look for the various free options available. These are good to get you started and they will get you off Excel. Yes, Excel is a great program for sorting and analysing data (and all kinds of other good things) but it is not the best tool for holding your data for any length of time. Excel spreadsheets get old, fast. Why? Because spreadsheets don't get updated or we lose track of the most up-to-date version. Or someone takes it home on their laptop and it's lost forever.

This stage is about looking at what you have and considering if you need something better—so really consider how you will store / manage the data you will need to use for your fundraising strategy.

A unique and irreplaceable donor engagement experience: This is a resource you may not have thought much about. Consider if you have an opportunity to share your work with donors in a way they won't or can't experience with any other organisation. Perhaps you have emotional videos or photographs or even physical ways to show a donor your work in action.

Here's a true example of a unique donor engagement experience:

Zoos Victoria, 150th Anniversary Campaign

The aim was to share the benefits of a zoo as a centre for conservation. Working with the carnivore keepers at Melbourne Zoo, I took a group of potential donors—quite literally—into the lion's den (the lions were safely in their enclosure at the time). The donors ran around putting out food for the lions and then returned to safety before the lions were released. During the time the donors were inside the fence (and they were never at risk), the lions were roaring to get to their dinner. I've never seen donors move so fast. Did they have an amazing experience that could not be delivered any other way? Yes! Did they donate? You bet they did, and they invited all of their friends to have the experience too. That's a unique, irreplaceable donor engagement opportunity. They had a story to tell over dinner—one that couldn't be beaten.

What could you offer your donors that would be unique and irreplaceable?

4.3 Time

We all have too little of this resource. Your fundraising strategy can stretch across six months, one year or up to three years. While you may have 12 months to implement your strategy, you will hope to see returns along the way. At this stage, you are considering when you need to show results; when your manager or board expect (or need) to see a return on your investment; and whether you have a week or a year or three years to achieve your fundraising goals.

If your goal is truly urgent, for example, you need to respond to an environmental disaster, you will need to throw all your resources at the issue to achieve your goal. If you can extend your deadline, you may be able to engage in activities that have a longer turnaround time.

Value / time commitment with donations: Not all donation strategies are equal in terms of how long it takes to raise funds. You need more gifts from more donors if the size of their average gift is small. The reverse is true if the average gift is larger because you'll need fewer donors.

As can be seen in the graph below, smaller gifts can be acquired faster than larger gifts; however, you need to talk to and convert far more people to attract lots of smaller gifts.

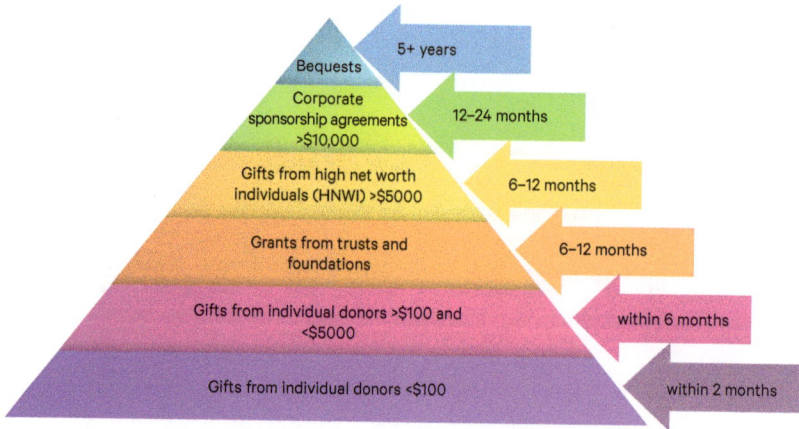

As you can see, it can take *less* time to attract individual donations of under $100; however, you will need many individual donations to achieve your goal; therefore, you will end up investing time and money to attract more small donors.

Trust and foundation applications take more time than money. You need to invest time to find the right grant opportunities and make multiple applications before you are successful.

Donations above $5,000 also take time and require you to identify the donors and build relationships.

Bequests take the longest time because you must wait until the donor has died before you can receive the donation; however, individual gifts can be significant and are therefore worth waiting for.

Be clear on your timeframe: When it comes to the time allowed for a strategy, a word of caution—there is a difference between a project that is 'important' and one that is 'urgent'. Make sure you are not getting caught up in an 'urgency' trap. If you feel you have no time to conduct your fundraising strategy, you may be tempted to cut corners or give up. Also, ignore those who tell you, 'We must have the money today'. If that really is the case, you don't need a fundraising strategy, you need a miracle (and that takes longer).

4.4 Money

Money. That's what we're here for, right? There are two categories of money that we will talk about here: **expenditure** and **income**. You need one to get the other.

To implement your strategy, you will need some level of financial investment. If you have zero dollars to spend, you will raise less than you otherwise might (or nothing at all). The more limited the money you can invest, the longer it will take to implement your strategy and show results. You don't need a huge expenditure budget but you will need 'some' funds. You will need to create an income and expenditure budget. You will want to measure your return and the only way to do this is to know how much you spent and how much you earned.

Your fundraising expenditure budget: Every strategy needs some money and all fundraising costs something to implement (in time, people or dollars). No matter how little you have, whether it's $50 or $50,000, you need to document it.

The more urgently the funds are needed, the more money, focused time and resources you will need to invest in your fundraising to achieve your goal. There is no such thing as fast, free income.

Knowing how much you have available to spend will do at least two things: it will help define what you can pay for and it will help measure your return on investment (ROI).

Achieving a return on investment (ROI): When you invest time, resources and money into fundraising, you want to achieve a positive

ROI, otherwise, what's the point? While you may make friends along the way, develop relationships and build donor engagement, the primary purpose of your strategy is to raise funds. Plus, you may want to raise more than you spend.

$$ROI = \frac{\text{Net return on investment}}{\text{Cost of investment}} \times 100\%$$

When you divide the net amount you generate by the amount you invest—that is your fundraising ROI. So if you invest $50,000 to raise a net of $100,000, your ROI is 200%.

There will be times when you will invest more than you will gain in the short or even long term. Not all approaches deliver funds straight away. Bequests or legacies are good examples. You may invest in staff, systems and donor engagement for many years before you see a return on your investment but the ultimate return can be very high. Therefore, this understanding needs to inform your strategy.

Your fundraising income target: This is the amount of money you need to raise. At this point you may be thinking *I need to raise as much as possible*. It may be challenging and a bit scary but you need to have a specific goal. You could set a goal based on what you have raised in the past, for example, a 10% increase on last year. You could also set a target based on what you know about the project or projects you need to fund. You could commit to raising funds for a certain percentage of those projects.

If you are raising money for a building, you should conduct a feasibility study to help you understand the potential for raising the funds you need. Feasibility studies are covered in a later section.

Make your target as specific as possible so that you can measure it and be assured that you have achieved it.

Set annual fundraising targets: Once you have a degree of clarity around how much is needed to implement the work, you can set fundraising targets for the year or the next few years. Usually a three-year target is the maximum time frame and even then, you'll need to review it every year.

Don't worry if your goal is $10,000 or $1 million; just set it. You can change it later if it turns out to be too ambitious or not ambitious enough. If you don't have a history of fundraising, you may want to set a conservative goal that you are more likely to achieve rather than setting a big, audacious goal that you may not meet. Meeting goals gives confidence so bear this in mind when you set your goals.

In most of my executive roles, the fundraising targets were set before I'd even started in the job and were usually decided based on not much evidence. If you do not have the luxury of setting your own fundraising target, you can still ensure that you understand how realistic your targets are. Start by capturing and analysing your organisation's previous three years of income to understand what percentage of the total revenue comes from fundraising income. Is this year's fundraising goal consistent or reasonable compared to past results? If the fundraising goal is significantly higher this year, can you get an explanation about why the target has increased? Have you requested more resources to help deliver them?

If your internal donation history is not easy to access, look to your organisation's published annual report. Most organisations will produce an annual report on all income and expenditure. Ask your friendly finance team for a copy of the previous year's annual report. You can then use this data to see whether your current fundraising goal is realistic or not.

To summarise, you will deliver more if you are clear on your goal. You can be more confident about your goal if you know what resources you have to back you. Always create an income and expenditure budget— no matter how small your budget, no matter how little you think you have to spend. You cannot measure what you don't record. If it matters, measure it. So write it down.

Step 5: Analysing donors and prospects

We now look at what types of donors and prospects we have available right now. Later we will look at how to attract new prospects. Here you want to identify how many of each you have. You probably want more donors, but at this stage, we are looking at your current resources.

5.1 Existing donors and prospects

Essentially there are two categories to consider. Past donors are those who have donated to you before and prospects are those who might donate to you when asked.

Past donors

Who has donated to you previously and do you want to attract similar donors in the future (prospects)? If your organisation is new, you may not have previous donors, so you'll need to consider from whom you want to raise funds.

Donors will fall into one of three categories as we talked about before:

- Individual donors (giving small and large gifts).
- Institutional donors (trusts and foundations giving grants).
- Corporate sponsors (giving sponsorships or corporate grants).

Most of your fundraising income will come from individual donors who will fall into one of three categories of financial donors:

- Those who donated within the last three years (current donors).
- Those who donated more than three years ago (lapsed donors).
- Those who have never donated to you (prospects).

Capture how many donors or prospects you have and this gives you a benchmark. The fewer donors you have, the more your strategy will need to focus on acquisition of new donors (finding and converting prospects into donors).

You can use this template to capture what you know about your donors and prospects. If you have a CRM system or database, you may be able to run donor reports to give you this information. If your records are less than reliable, make a good estimate to give you an idea of where you stand.

	Type of donor (Individual, corporate or institutional)	Quantity (number of donors, prospects, lapsed)	Quantity with an address	Quantity with a contact number	Quantity with an email address	Quantity with no contact information
Donor: Gave in the past 3 years						
Lapsed donor: Has not given in the past 3 years but has given in the past						
Prospect: Never given						

Here you are capturing broad data. How many do you have of each category and what information do you have about them? This will help you determine your fundraising strategy.

5.2 Developing demographic donor profiles

Now you have an idea of how many of what type of donor / prospect you have, add to your understanding by answering some demographic questions based on information you already have:

	Category	Why?
1.	Age	Once you capture the date of birth of your prospects and donors, you can work out their age. A database with a younger average age (<25 years old) will require a different communications approach to a database with older donors (>65 years old). Capturing your donors' date of birth is good practice as it can help identify donors with the same name.
2.	Gender	Do you have more women or men on your database? Research shows that women give more often and men give larger gifts. This may affect your approach in your fundraising strategy.[8]
3.	Location (State and country)	Where are your donors based? Do they live in major cities or in regional centres? This information can help you decide, for example, whether running face-to-face events in major cities is a good idea.
4.	Postcode	Postcode research is available to help you understand whether your donors live in wealthy suburbs; this may indicate their capacity to give larger gifts. You can also test direct mail communications to particular postcodes or suburbs.
5.	Marital / Family status	It is helpful to know your donors' marital status in order to address them correctly. In addition, when combined with age data, you can determine whether your donor is a bequest prospect (a single or widowed older woman >75 years) or a young, single person <25 years who may be interested in more active events like a sponsored bike ride. Donors give different amounts when they are at different stages of their lives: a young couple with young children and a big mortgage may donate less than an older single woman with no children and a high disposable income.
6.	Employment status	If your donors will tell you whether they are retired or still working, this can substitute for age data. Also, you may suggest different types of engagement activities or fundraising requests if you know that someone is no longer employed. Also, tax deductibility can be less of an issue for someone who is not working and therefore does not have a taxable salary.

Recency, frequency, value and size of gift

On the assumption that you have some donors (and if you don't, please don't worry we will get onto donor acquisition very soon), let's now look at further categorising our donors and prospects.

If you have their donor history you can look at their behaviours in terms of recency, frequency, value and size of gift. We deal with each of these below. With current and lapsed donors, you can segment them by these measures to help determine their likelihood of giving again and the potential size of their future gift.

	Question	Why?
1.	**Recency: When did they last donate to you?**	This is a measure of when a donor last gave to you: Was it a week, a month or a year ago? The more recently they gave, the more likely they are to donate again especially if you have done a good job of thanking them for their original donation. The best time to ask a donor for a donation is soon after they have just given.
		It is important to know when your donor last donated to you so you know when to ask again. Practice shows that the best time to ask for a second or subsequent donation is right after the most recent one. If you know when they last gave to you, you can set up a plan to thank them effectively.
2.	**Frequency: How often do they donate to you?**	How often do they donate? Have they only donated once or more than once? Perhaps they are regular donors who donate every month or quarter? The frequency of their donation will help you understand when to ask again and how often to ask.
		Only 50% of donors give a second time; therefore, donors who make multiple gifts are those who really care about your organisation. Identifying these donors and recognising their generosity is an important part of donor care. Understanding why they give so frequently is useful to crafting your communications with them. What sorts of projects do they support? Why do they give at that particular frequency? If you understand this, you may find you can encourage other donors (who perhaps only gave once or twice) to give much more frequently.

	Question	Why?
3.	**Value: How much have they donated in total?**	How much have they donated in total? When you add up their total gifts, would you consider them a small or a major donor? The answer to this question may determine how you next contact them. Who is giving you the biggest gifts in total? You can look at individual gifts but also look at the total history of your donor. Did they give more or less in the past? Has the size of their donation changed? Has their frequency of donation changed? This information can help inform your fundraising approach.
4.	**Size: What was the size of their largest individual gift?**	80% of your income will come from 20% of your donors. This is the Pareto Principle, otherwise known as the '80:20 rule'. 80% of your income will come from people who give larger gifts and people who give often. You need to identify them and, in many cases, know them by name and have personal donor development plans for them. These are the people who keep your organisation going and you will be surprised how few of them there are.

5.3 Profiling and qualifying prospects

If you've never done any fundraising or have no donors, look to the people who started the organisation and the beneficiaries you are trying to help. What do they look like?

Fundraising—like charity—should begin at home, so look to the people closest to you and start with them. If it's just you, what do you look like? Who is most likely to support your cause? Are they people like you? Are they younger or older? Do they have the same demographic profile as you? If you don't know, look at similar organisations to yours (there will definitely be at least one other organisation with a similar mission).

Start with a profile and test whether or not it is the right one by asking them to help you. You won't know until you start fundraising. Don't put off fundraising because you're unsure who will donate. Develop a profile based on the criterion outlined above using the information you have available and get on with your strategy.

To qualify a prospective donor you must categorise them using the demographic and behavioural qualifications we used earlier. Use information like where they live, their age and their gender to determine if they 'look' like your current donors or people more likely to give to your type of cause.

Deciding who is most likely to donate

Those closest to you have the strongest links to your organisation but may or may not have the financial capacity to donate. In determining who is most likely to give, you can undertake an L.I.C. ranking. This determines who has the closest links, the most inclination to give and the financial capacity to give.

> **L:** They have a Link to the organisation. (They know someone in your organisation or they have a personal connection to your cause.)
>
> **I:** They are Inclined to donate. (They support causes like yours.)
>
> **C:** They have the Capacity to give at the level you would like. (They have the funds to give.)

There is a great temptation to focus on the third point exclusively. Remember, however, that having the capacity to support you in no way indicates that they *will* support you. And sometimes the greatest gifts come from those who, at face value, look like they have little to give.

As an example, let's look at the Bill & Melinda Gates Foundation. No one would doubt their capacity to give. And they do give. The Bill & Melinda Gates Foundation donates millions of dollars to a range of causes. But what is the likelihood that they would donate to your organisation?

Does their foundation support your type of cause? Does anyone in your organisation know them well enough that they would accept a call or email or a grant submission? For almost everyone, the Bill & Melinda Gates Foundation is a donor dream, not a bona fide prospect.

On the other hand, it is tempting to discount someone who does not look like they have the capacity to give, even if they have close ties to the organisation or care a lot about you. I often hear it said—incorrectly— that an organisation or long-term volunteers won't donate. It is often a mistake to ignore a group or individual because, in your view (based on little information), they are not 'wealthy enough'. Never assume, on someone else's behalf, whether they can or want to give to you. It is not up to the fundraiser to exclude someone who could be a wonderful donor and who would value the joy that giving brings to them. We must all learn to put aside our own prejudices and preconceived ideas, no matter how well meant, to allow others to make their own choices. We can only do this by allowing them the opportunity to give to the causes that are most important to them. And we can only do *this* by asking.

5.4 Donor acquisition

Do you want more new donors who look like your current donors? Or do you want different types of donors altogether? The next step is to write down what your prospective donors look like. The types of donors and the size of donation you are aiming to attract will help determine your fundraising strategy. Remember, all funding comes from four sources:

1. Individuals
2. Trusts and foundations
3. Government
4. Corporates.

Most donations come from individuals and that's why we focus on them so much. Individuals will give personal donations from $2.00 to millions of dollars. Some individuals will donate in order to receive a tax deduction; others will donate because they believe so firmly in the cause.

Individuals can be the source of legacies or bequests (donations left to an organisation in someone's will). These are not tax deductible as the donor must have died before the charity receives the legacy.

Individual donors can provide:

- one-off single gifts of any amount
- regular periodic gifts by direct debit arrangement
- multiple occasional gifts
- legacies or bequests.

One-off single gifts

Individual donors will make occasional gifts either in response to your fundraising requests or, less likely, of their own accord. Most donations happen because someone asked someone to donate. Unfortunately, statistics show that more than 50% of all donors to Australian charities and non-profit organisations only ever make one donation. According to the Association of Fundraising Professionals and the Center on Nonprofits and Philanthropy at the Urban Institute, the average donor retention rate in the USA after the first gift is around 45%. Australia's rate is 43%.[9] This means more than half of those who give will not give a second gift.

When you consider the cost to raise $1.00 and the organisational value of donor retention, it is clear that not-for-profits need to keep the donor at the centre of their communications to improve retention and get a better return on their fundraising investment.

Imagine doing all the work to create your fundraising strategy for a person to only ever make one donation. Your goal is to get them to give multiple times. That way, you build donor loyalty.

Regular periodic gifts by direct debit arrangement

One of the most effective methods for encouraging multiple gifts from a donor is to persuade them to set up a monthly direct debit for their donation. A regular periodic donor gives a small donation every month, sometimes for years. These donations mount up.

For example: If a regular donor commits to giving $10 a month by direct debit, that donor will give your organisation $120 a year or $360 over 3 years. If you had 1,000 of these donors, you will generate $120,000 every year (or $360,000 over three years). Once a direct debit arrangement is set up, you do not need to ask again—you just need to keep that donor happy. That is the power of a regular drip-feed of small donations particularly when multiplied across many donors.

If you can grow your regular giving program to attract a significant number of donors, you will have achieved several goals:

a. You will have converted many one-off donors into repeat donors.
b. You will have built a loyalty program by keeping your donors happy.
c. You will have delivered a **forecastable** income.

This last point is important. Fundraising income and donor behaviour can seem fickle and hard to forecast. Longer term, regular giving is highly forecastable as it is reliable. Once the program has been running for a number of years, trends emerge around attrition (the number of people leaving the program) and acquisition (the number of people joining the program). Once you understand these trends, you can forecast your income year to year. If you know for instance that 75% of your Year 1 regular donors are still giving five years later, you can forecast future income with considerable accuracy.

You can of course apply this logic to all donors but the main difference with regular donors is that they have committed to a mechanism (an automatic direct transfer usually from their credit card) that makes the gift 100% certain unless they cancel the arrangement.

Multiple occasional gifts

Occasional multi-gift donors are less easy to forecast unless, like the regular donor, they have set up a pattern of giving (for example, the donor always gives annually or quarterly). These donors deserve attention and personal consideration to understand what has stimulated them to give. Any donor who gives more than once is worthy of your attention.

Major donors can fit into this category whether they give individual gifts >$5,000 or a cumulative total of >$5,000. Paying attention to how donors donate as well as what stimulates them to donate is important information for your fundraising strategy.

Legacies or bequests

Bequests (also called legacies or gifts in wills) are donations left to your organisation by an individual donor in their will. You will only receive the funding after the donor's death. There are several reasons and benefits to encouraging your donors to leave a gift to your organisation in their will:

- A bequest can be large compared to your organisation's average donation. The current average bequest amount in Australia is around $40,000–$50,000.[10]
- With the rise in Australian house prices, an estate can be much larger at the end of a donor's life than at the time they wrote their will; therefore, if you are bequeathed the donor's home, the gift you receive can be considerable.

Consider this: In 1995, the median price for a house in Australia was $111,524 and an apartment was $123,840. By 2020, the median national value of a house in Australia grew by 412% and apartments by 316% with the median national property price now $549,918. Research predicts that by 2043 and with an average annual rise of 8.6%, the national median house value could be close to $3 million and apartments could be valued at $2.3 million.[11] It could make a big difference for your organisation if someone bequeathed you a house they purchased pre-1995.

A bequest is a good choice for a donor who is 'asset rich' but 'cash poor'. For example, they cannot afford to give during their lifetime but could make a gift from their estate. Imagine if everyone on your board or management committee left a bequest to your organisation and the impact that would have over future years.

Time, talent and treasure

A last thought on who should give and where to find more money. Your board of trustees, subcommittee members, staff, volunteers and past donors—even your management team—have the closest connections to your organisation and should be asked to donate. These people care enough about your organisation to give their time. You will still need to establish their capacity to give, but rest assured, they *will* have a capacity to give something according to their own individual means if they care enough about the cause.

I do not support the view that because someone donates their 'time and talent' that they cannot also donate 'treasure', i.e. make a financial donation. The most successful organisations have governing boards and committees who give all three. These are exactly the people who should be asked to financially donate to the organisation. The USA charities have a phrase for this: you can 'give, get or get off the board'. Harsh but necessary.

Everyone on the board, council, executive team and / or fundraising committee should donate. Why should your donors give to your organisation if you don't? Everyone in a leadership position in your organisation should donate at a level at which they can. Not everyone can make a $10,000 donation or even a $1,000 donation but almost everyone can make some level of donation even $10 a month. There is great power when you, as the fundraiser, can say with your hand on your heart, 'Everyone on our board has donated to our cause'.

SUMMARY

Now you should have a written document that begins to clarify:

- the resources available to you—people, tools, time and money
- how much money you have to invest (your expenditure budget)
- how much you need to raise and for what projects (your income target)
- the types of donors you want to attract
- what your ROI should look like.

You are well on your way to imagining what your fundraising strategy will look like. It's time to move to the next stage: Write your fundraising strategy.

Stage 2

Write your fundraising strategy

'Philanthropy is not just about money ... it is about using whatever resources you have ... and applying them to improve the world.'

—Melinda Gates

WRITE YOUR FUNDRAISING STRATEGY

In Stage 1, you collected the background information needed to write your fundraising strategy. In Stage 2, you will focus on steps 6–10 and you will make the strategic decisions about what you want to achieve and how you will make the best use of the resources you have available.

You will capture these decisions in your fundraising strategy template. This is where you clarify how you will go about achieving your fundraising targets using your available resources and tools.

4-STAGE FUNDRAISING STRATEGY		
STEP	**DESCRIPTION**	**YOUR PROGRESS**
Stage 2: Write your fundraising strategy		
6	Strategic approach and competitive advantage	
7	Your unique selling proposition (USP)	
8	SMART goals and objectives	
9	Determine your target audience/s 9.1 Turning suspects into advocates: the Ladder of Loyalty 9.2 The donor pyramid 9.3 Donor retention and growth	
10	Fundraising income and expenditure budget 10.1 Budget by type of donor 10.2 Budget by marketing channel 10.3 Determine your net return	

Step 6: Strategic approach and competitive advantage

In order to achieve your goals, you need a strategic approach. Your strategic approach will help to deliver on your financial goals.

Strategy is <u>not</u> the same as a goal or an objective. Your strategy is the approach you will take to achieve your goals; therefore, you will likely have one strategy and multiple goals.

If you want to gain more insights into strategy, I recommend reading two books by the brilliant strategist, Dr Michael Porter: *Competitive Advantage* and *On Competition*.[12] In both books, Porter discusses commercial rather than non-profit organisations; however, his concepts are useful to any organisation. You can aim for competitive advantage as a non-profit by becoming more agile and more effective in how you use donor funds and what you achieve with those funds. In other words, you can choose to be different from your competitors.

An example: When I was Chief Marketing Officer at Plan International, we had a major competitor in a very large faith-based child sponsorship agency. Plan International chose a strategic approach to differentiate itself as a secular child sponsorship agency focused on outcomes for women and girls, something our competitor could not. While Plan was a smaller entity than its competitor, it achieved exceptional growth by taking this position and building its brand around it as it attracted those who saw this positioning as an asset. Plan did not aspire to be number one but it was a much stronger number two in the market.

Dr Porter describes three generic strategies that apply to all industries and can be used to set your organisation apart from its competition. They are Cost Leadership, Differentiation (creating unique products and services) and Focus (offering a specialised service in particular parts of the markets). Charities must differentiate themselves from their 'competitors': other charities, schools, universities and all the other charitable activities that donors could spend their money on. Price or cost is not a leverage point as charities are not 'selling' a product and, therefore, donations cannot be cheaper or more expensive than other charities. However, a charity can focus on providing greater 'value'. How much does the donor value the work of your charity? How much does the donor love your work and your cause? How much do you show your love and appreciation for the donors? A charity that consistently and authentically thanks and acknowledges its donors can really use this as a point of difference.

A charity can focus on delivering specific services to particular market segments so there is an opportunity to differentiate by focus. BirdLife Australia is an example of a charity that offers unique operations to specifically help protect Australian and international bird species from extinction by protecting habitats and advocating for better nature laws. This focus attracts donors (like me) who care about birds and their habitats. This differentiates them from a broader 'animal charity' that protects a wider selection of flora and fauna. Consider how you can position your organisation with potential donors and link into their interests.

Step 7: Your unique selling proposition (USP)

Your USP is what makes you different from other organisations or causes. Why should anyone want to donate to support your cause? How can you narrow down your offering into a compelling statement? You could consider this your 'elevator pitch' and it forms part of your Case for Support. It's a specific benefit that makes your organisation or cause stand out when compared to other organisations in your community or the wider market. If it takes three pages to give this 'elevator pitch', it's two and a half pages too long and you haven't thought about it hard enough. Keep working on it until it's down to a paragraph, or better yet, one sentence. Consider a few of these examples:

a. **Australian Red Cross** is building a better society based on people helping people.

b. **World Vision** is a child-focused charity organisation. With Australians' support, we tackle poverty and transform lives through development, relief and advocacy.

c. **Hobsons Bay Wetlands Centre** is a place where everyone can connect with nature to improve health and wellbeing and be inspired to care for our precious natural environment.

Your statement must mean something to the donor, not just to the staff or volunteers of your organisation. Your USP will inform the fundraising materials you will produce to raise funds.

It can take a long time and lots of 'group editing' to get a USP right. If you have an agreed USP, use it. If you don't, do your best to write a brief sentence that describes what makes your organisation different or appealing to your target audiences.

Step 8: SMART goals and objectives

Vagueness is the enemy of effective fundraising. In order to clarify how to approach your fundraising, decide where you want to end up. What is your goal? What is your destination? You need to create SMART goals so you know when you've achieved your objectives.

Statements like, 'I want to raise lots of money' or 'I want more donors' are not goals—they are wishes. They cannot be targeted with any level of measurability. How many 'more donors' or how much money is 'lots'? You need a specific destination. You need to create goals. You can only choose your path when you know where you want to end up, and you can only measure your success if you have set a goal.

Create SMART goals

SMART goals can be measured. They will help you decide where you want to go and what success looks like for you. You can apply the SMART goal principle to any type of goal setting.

A SMART goal is:

Specific: It is not vague or woolly.

Measurable: You can measure whether you have achieved it.

Actionable: It can be actioned.

Realistic: It is something your organisation can do.

Time bound: It has a clear delivery time frame and deadline.

You will likely have two kinds of goals or objectives: financial and non-financial.

A financial goal is how much money you want to raise, from which donors and by when?

A non-financial goal may be the number of new donors you want to acquire or the percentage of prospects you want to convert.

I want to raise more money than last year is not a SMART goal. If you raise $1.00 more, it could be considered a success, but it's probably not what you were aiming for. You could make it a SMART goal by clarifying how much you raised last year, by how much you want to increase the goal (10%) and by when.

Another example: *I want to raise $100,000 from individual donors giving $20 a month by November 2025* is a specific, measurable, time bound goal. This is what you are aiming for and you will know whether you have achieved this goal.

Writing down a goal does not mean you will achieve it, but without a clear goal you have no way of knowing if you have achieved it or reached your chosen destination. So consider where you want to go with your fundraising activity.

ACTION: Create a SMART goal (or a series of SMART goals) for your fundraising activities. What do you want to achieve? How much do you want to raise? Be specific. How many donors do you need? What projects do you want funding for and how much will they cost to implement? The more detail the better. You can always amend your goal(s) but get into the habit of creating SMART goals that you can measure.

An example of a SMART financial goal: *We will raise $100,000 from individual donors and foundations by December 2025.*

An example of a SMART strategic goal: *We will achieve this financial goal by attracting three new grants of $5,000 each and 850 donors to give a minimum donation of $100 each.*

Now you know what you are trying to achieve. You have written specific goals and you can share these with the stakeholders and agree that this is where you are going. If they don't agree or think you are being too ambitious or not ambitious enough, again, now is a good time to have that discussion.

In order to write a SMART goal, you will have thought through why this is the right goal for you at this time, for example, because your organisation has never raised more than $50,000 or because your bequest program is going really well. The benefit of setting SMART goals is that you are forced to do the thinking to support your argument for the right SMART goals.

Step 9: Determine your target audience/s

In the earlier stages, you have spent time considering whether you have any current or past donors and what they look like. You will also have thought about how to find new donors and keep your current donors giving long into the future.

9.1 Turning suspects into advocates: the Ladder of Loyalty

When you consider your target audiences, think about how you want to 'move' your donors through the organisation. Here you will consider your contacts' levels of loyalty. Suspects are people who don't know about your organisation or why they should support it. They have no loyalty to you. Using research and qualification, you can turn suspects into prospects—those who know about you but are not yet convinced to donate. There is no loyalty here yet either. Through further qualification and cultivation, you can convert prospects into donors because you have started to develop the relationship and build loyalty. If you steward the relationship well, you convert donors into advocates. They do not only donate multiple times but they encourage others to donate. These are your most loyal donors.

This process is sometimes called 'moves management', where you move the donor through the different stages of identification, qualification, cultivation and stewardship. It can also be called the Donor Ladder of Loyalty. As the donor learns more about the organisation, and if they like what they see, their loyalty grows. You want to create a strategy to ensure *suspects become prospects become donors become advocates*. Advocates are your ultimate donors. Think of the Donor Ladder of Loyalty as your way of turning your donors into raving fans.

Donor Ladder of Loyalty

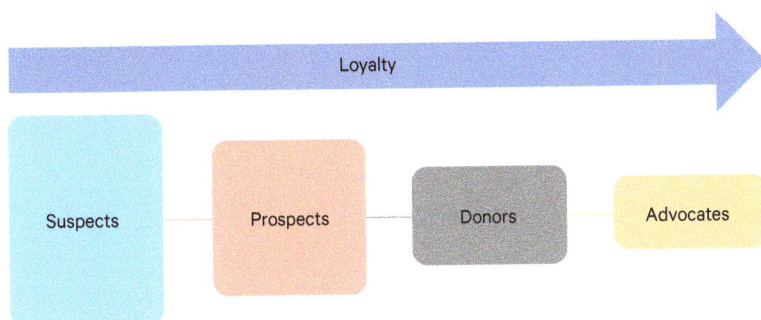

Understanding the size of individual gifts you want to attract

In determining your target audience, you should consider the size and type of gifts you want to attract: the bigger the gift, the more personalised your fundraising approach should be as you will likely be asking high net worth individuals (donors with more disposable income).

The greater the number of large donations you can attract, the fewer donors you will need to acquire to meet your goal. As an example, let's say you want to raise $10,000 as in the table below. You could find four donors (after considering possibly 40 prospects) to each give $2,500. This will take a personalised approach probably with one-to-one engagement. If you take another approach, say, to attract 100 donors to give $100 each, you may need to find >1,000 prospects to convert to donors and you may contact them using more broader marketing methods. Why do you need so many prospects? Because not everyone you ask will donate.

Strategic approach	Target to be raised	Number of prospects	Number of donors	Size of individual gift	Amount raised
Personalised (one-on-one engagement)	$10,000	40	4	$2,500	$10,000
Broad marketing	$10,000	1,000	100	$100	$10,000

Knowing the size of donation you want to attract will determine the fundraising approach you will take and the amount of investment you will need to apply to attract those donations. Your approach will be determined by those resources we discussed: people, tools, time and money. Having said this, we know that most donations come from individuals:

- Individuals who make small gifts (less than $5,000).
- Individuals who make big gifts (more than $5,000).

Smaller donors may give an individual donation of up to $5,000. Major donors will give above $5,000 as organisations often set their definition of major donors as those who give a $5,000 donation and above. You can choose your definition of a small and major donor.

Individual donors can be approached through mass media channels (TV, radio, billboards, email) or via personalised approaches (face-to-face meetings). However, the larger the gift you are targeting, the more likely you will use personalised approaches.

As you work through this book, you will see that the larger the donation you are aiming for, the less money you will need to spend on fundraising activities to attract that donation. How's that for a piece of good luck? However, larger donations require more engagement, energy, time and people resources.

Large donations can come from high net worth individuals (HNWI). In order to solicit a donation from them, you will need to take a personalised approach. You may support this type of solicitation with other marketing activities but in order to get the gift, you'll need to 'personally' ask for it rather than sending a direct mail pack or an email.

Your budget will reflect the type of fundraising activities you intend to invest in. This will, in turn, reflect the size and type of donations you want to generate. You also want to think about the particular types of donors you want to attract so you can match your channels with your donors.

9.2 The donor pyramid

Earlier we mentioned the Pareto Principle or the 80:20 rule. It states that in many cases, 80% of any results come from 20% of the cause of those results. This applies in fundraising too. It is likely that 80% or more of your income will come from 20% or less of your donors. It's therefore useful to be able to identify those donors who are likely to give you most of your income. We can view this as the donor pyramid. In the diagram below, we can see that the largest donations are at the top and come from the smallest number of donors or sources. At the other end are the smaller donations and they come from the largest number of people. In this way, we see that the majority of our income, as we move up the pyramid, comes from the smallest number of donors.

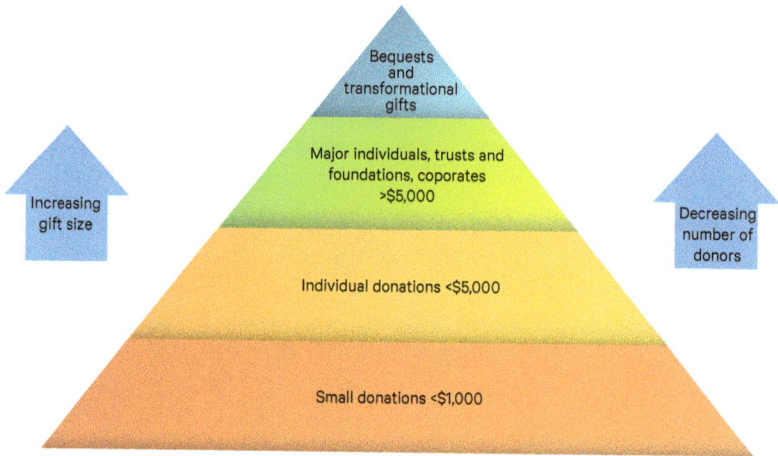

So if your strategy is to attract small sized donations, you will need more donors to achieve your goal. And if you want to focus on large sized donations, you will need fewer donors to achieve your goal.

As we've discussed, the larger the gift you want to attract, the more you will rely on face-to-face and personal engagement with individual donors or trusts. The smaller the gift, the more you will rely on mass or direct marketing methods to generate donations from large numbers of prospects. This gives us three types of fundraising approaches:

- Volume: Talking to many prospects to attract donors.
- Personalised: Talking to a few qualified prospects to attract donors.
- Combination: Combining volume and a personalised approach to attract donors.

Type of donor	Volume approach	Personalised approach	Combination approach
Investment required	$$$, resources	$, time	$$, resources and time
Individual donors giving <$100	X		
Individual donors giving >$5,000 and bequests		X	X
Trusts and foundation		X	
Corporations		X	
Speed of acquisition of donor	Fast	Slow	Medium

Volume approach (large number of donors / smaller donations): The bottom of the donor pyramid shows the majority of donors give small donations of less than $1,000. According to the *Giving in Australia 2016 Report,* roughly 15 million Australians donated $12.5 billion to charities and not-for-profit (NFP) organisations in 2015–16, with a median donation of A$200.[13] These donors require a 'volume' approach. You will need to talk to a lot of *prospective* donors (prospects) to convert a percentage of them into *actual* donors.

Personalised approach (small number of donors / larger donations): Major donors (those giving more than $5,000) at the top of the pyramid *can* be attracted through a volume fundraising approach but more often require a personalised approach. Larger donors require a lower level of financial investment as their cultivation relies mainly on the resources of time to build relationships and people to help cultivate these relationships and encourage larger donations.

Bequests and transformational gifts: Bequests take the longest amount of time to turn into actual donations (five years or more).

Bequests require one of the lowest levels of financial investment but, again, require the time and talent of people to cultivate relationships. Transformational gifts are those that literally transform your organisation either because of their size (usually) or because they fund any vital area of operations that could not have happened in any other way. These types of gifts take considerable time and an orchestrated effort across the organisation to achieve.

So which groups would you target if:

- you are in a hurry to raise funds?
- you have limited funds to invest?
- you have limited human resources?

9.3 Donor retention and growth

To build your database of donors, you'll need a combination of acquisition (new donors) and retention (holding on to existing donors). If you go for acquisition only and do not think about growing the percentage of donors giving more than once (retention), you may spend a lot of money at the top of your funnel only to have few donors to show for it after three to five years.

Without a retention strategy (holding on to your donors so they continue to be loyal and donate), you will have a hole in your bucket. This means that as quickly as you find new donors, they will drop out the bottom— they will stop giving. Effectively, a donor who only gives once has left your organisation. They are not loyal.

Look at the strategic approach you want to take as well as the tactics you want to use. Here are some key levers that maximise retention of donors.

Fundraising levers

There are several fundraising levers you can apply to increase the amount of money you raise. In the following examples, I show you how they build on each other to increase your overall fundraising income.

Lever 1: Increase the size of your average donation.

Lever 2: Increase the percentage of donors giving again via retention.

Lever 3: Increase the number of donors each year via acquisition.

Once you have attracted your donor's first donation, your aim should be to:

1. increase the size of individual gifts from those donors
2. get a second and subsequent gift from existing donors
3. acquire new donors.

With this approach, you are lifting everyone up the Ladder of Loyalty with larger gifts more often. This is how you grow your income and your donor base.

Let's look at how these objectives build on each other using the assumption that each year only 50% of donors give again. In reality, it is likely that even fewer of your donors will give each year if you don't take any action but let's use this as an example.

The baseline case

Let's say you hold an event and that attracts 400 new donors to your organisation in Year 0. You do nothing else after that event except ask for another donation each year.

Therefore, the following is a possible scenario:

1. The organisation does not increase or decrease the size of the average gift in year 0.

2. Only 50% of the previous year's donors give again (are retained) the next year.

3. The organisation does not attract more donors in subsequent years 1, 2 and 3 (no acquisition).

BASELINE CASE					
Year	Year 0	Year 1	Year 2	Year 3	TOTAL $
Number of donors	400	200	100	50	
Average donation	$100	$100	$100	$100	
Total money raised	$40,000	$20,000	$10,000	$5,000	**$75,000**

In the baseline case, you can see that over three years, income steadily falls as the number of active donors also declines. This example represents a declining donor base. By the end of Year 3, only 12.5% (50 donors) of the 400 donors you started with are still donating. This is a common situation after an initial burst of enthusiasm because the organisation has failed to look after its current donors or attract new donors. So $75,000 is generated in total.

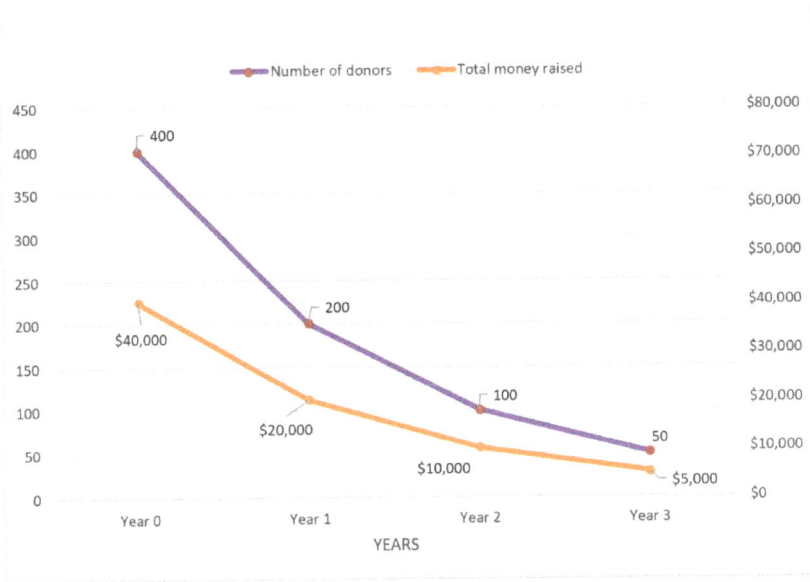

Graph 1: Baseline Case

So what can we do about this? Let's look at several scenarios firstly using each of the three levers and then scenarios with the levers used in combination:

Scenario 1: Lever 1: Increase the size of your average donation

Let's use the baseline case and start with 400 donors at Year 0. We will now:

1. increase the average donation by $10 each year for Years 1, 2 and 3
2. retain 50% of the previous year's donors to donate again
3. acquire no new donors.

We can see the impact that increasing the annual gift has on annual and total donations.

SCENARIO 1: Increase the average gift by $10 each year					
Year	Year 0	Year 1	Year 2	Year 3	TOTAL $
Number of donors	400	200	100	50	
Average donation	$100	$110	$120	$130	
Total money raised	$40,000	$22,000	$12,000	$6,500	$80,500

As you see in the charts, the total amount raised increases by $5,500 to $80,500 compared with the baseline case total of $75,000; however, the number of donors still decreases by 50% each year as no new donors are added. This means we are getting more money from each donor, but overall, the donor base is still declining. This is unsustainable as you'll need to squeeze more from fewer donors as time goes on, so this needs to be addressed.

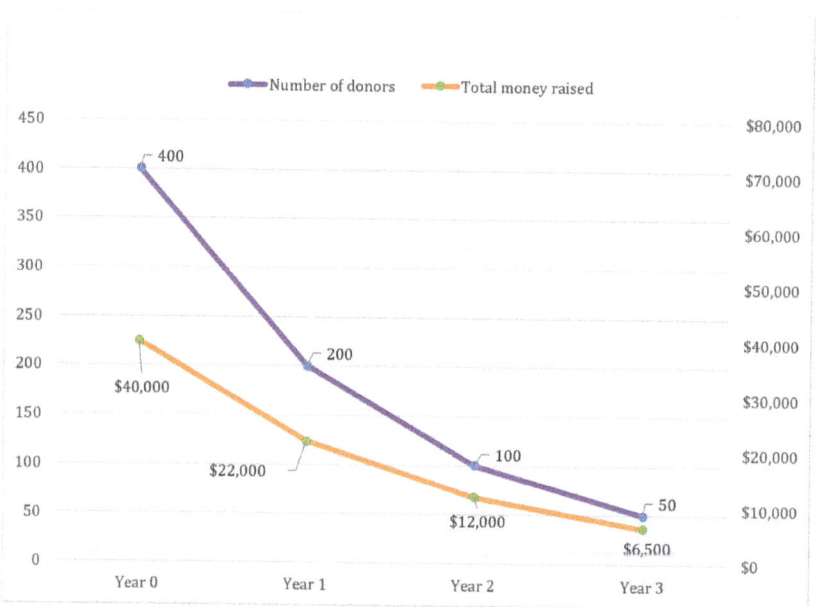

Graph 2: Scenario 1: Lever 1 – Increase the size of the average donation

Scenario 2: Lever 2: Improve retention

In sales, there is a truism that it costs ten times more to attract a new customer than it does to keep an existing one. This is true of donors as well. It is always a better investment to invest in retaining more of your current donors as it is more expensive to attract new ones. With retention, you are trying to increase the number of donors who give more than once, i.e. you want to improve loyalty.

If we go back to our base case, we have 400 donors. In this scenario we:

1. maintain the average gift at $100
2. retain 70% of the previous year's donors to give again (compared with 50%)
3. acquire no new donors.

Let's see what that does to our results:

SCENARIO 2: Improve Retention					
Year	Year 0	Year 1	Year 2	Year 3	TOTAL $
Number of donors	400	280	196	137	
Average donation	$100	$100	$100	$100	
Total money raised	$40,000	$28,000	$19,600	$13,720	$101,320

So without acquiring any new donors, total income by Year 3 has increased from the baseline scenario from $75,000 to over $101,000 just by retaining more donors—in this scenario, we have 137 donors still giving by the end of the third year. This is the power of retention. However, donor numbers are still declining, just at a slower rate, so we will want to counter this.

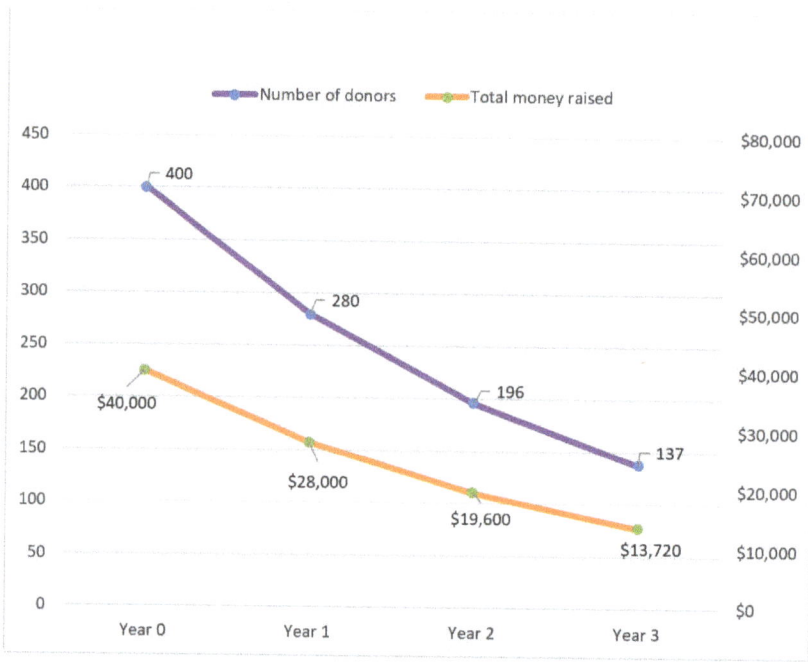

Graph 3: Scenario 2: Lever 2 – Improve retention

Scenario 3: Lever 3: Acquire new donors

So you may think we should acquire new donors. Let's look at a scenario where we do just this and:

1. maintain the average gift at $100

2. retain 50% of the previous year's donors to donate again

3. use our fundraising skills to acquire 200 new donors each year.

SCENARIO 3: Acquire new donors					
Year	Year 0	Year 1	Year 2	Year 3	TOTAL $
Existing donors	400	200	100	50	
Year 1		200	100	50	

Year 2			200	100	
Year 3				200	
Total donors per year	400	400	400	400	
Average donation	$100	$100	$100	$100	
Total money raised	$40,000	$40,000	$40,000	$40,000	**$160,000**

This is, in fact, a stagnant database where we just replace the donors we've lost. However, our income increases substantially from the baseline scenario of $75,000 as we have, through acquisition, maintained the number of donors who donate each year at 400. So each year we generate $40,000 giving a total of $160,000 at the end of Year 3. We also need to check whether our ROI is sufficient for this situation to be acceptable, i.e. how much we need to invest in order to deliver this return.

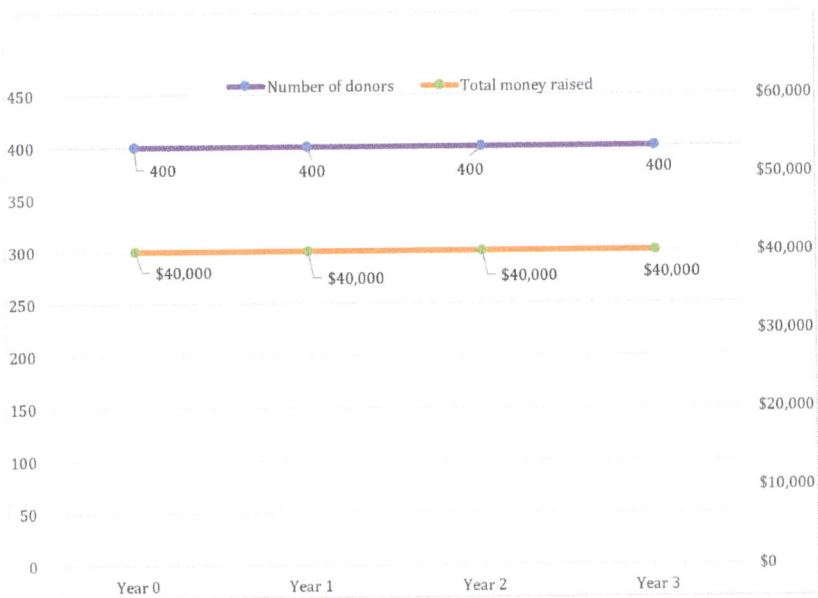

Graph 4: Scenario 3: Lever 3 – Acquisition of new donors each year

Using the levers in combination

We can of course use these levers in combination. With these scenarios, we start to see growth and our income is becoming more sustainable. So let's look at some scenarios where we combine the different levers.

Scenario 4: Levers 1+3 (combined): Increase the average gift and acquire new donors

In this scenario, we use two levers to improve our results and:

1. increase the average donation by $10 each year
2. retain 50% of the previous year's donors to donate again (as before)
3. increase the number of donors through acquisition by 400 donors per year which more than offsets our losses through attrition.

SCENARIO 4: Increase the average gift by $10 a year and acquire new donors					
Year	Year 0	Year 1	Year 2	Year 3	TOTAL $
Existing donors	400	200	100	50	
Year 1		400	200	100	
Year 2			400	200	
Year 3				400	
Total Donors per year	400	600	700	750	
Average Donation	$100	$110	$120	$130	
Total money raised	$40,000	$66,000	$84,000	$97,500	**$287,500**

As you will see in the chart, using two levers has the effect of growing the number of donors year on year, offsetting our 50% attrition and increasing overall income because the size of the average gift increases.

As 50% of our new donors donate the next year, we move them into existing donors. Now we are starting to see growth in our database. Compared with the baseline scenario, total income has increased to $287,500—a substantial increase.

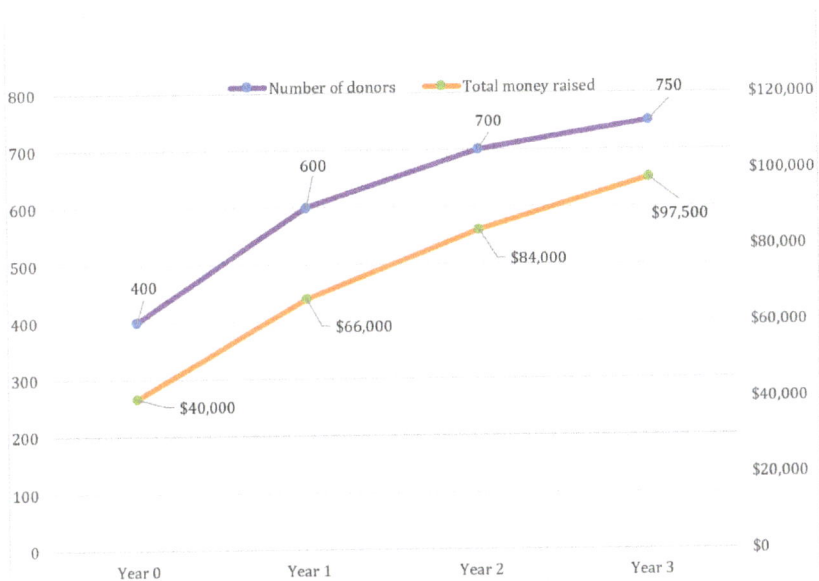

Graph 5: Scenario 4: Lever 1 + 3

In our final scenario, we will bring all three levers together:

Scenario 5: Levers 1+2+3 (Combined): Increase the average gift, improve retention and acquire new donors

This is the trifecta scenario where we combine all the levers. We will look at what happens when we:

1. increase the average gift by $10 per annum

2. increase the percentage of the previous year's donors from 50% (in our earlier scenarios) to 70%

3. increase the number of donors by 400 a year.

Year	Year 0	Year 1	Year 2	Year 3	TOTAL $
SCENARIO 5: Levers 1+2+3 (combined): Acquire new donors, increase the average gift and improve retention					
Existing donors	400	280	196	137	
Year 1		400	280	196	
Year 2			400	280	
Year 3				400	
Total donors per year	400	680	876	1,013	
Average donation	$100	$110	$120	$130	
Total money raised	$40,000	$74,800	$105,120	$131,716	**$351,636**

In Scenario 5, we have a thriving database. We are retaining more of our donors—70% give again the next year; our average gift has increased to $130 by Year 3; and our total income has increased to $351,636 by Year 3—a massive increase on our baseline scenario of $75,000. Importantly, we have a more engaged, growing supporter base and we are learning how to use the fundraising levers to grow income and increase loyalty.

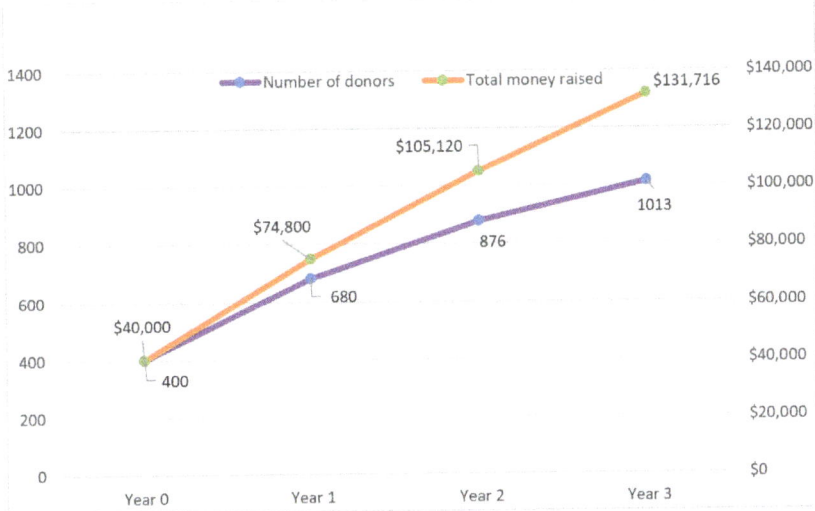

Graph 6: Scenario 5: Lever 1 + 2+ 3

Consider which levers you can action

In summary, you should use a combination of these levers to maintain and grow your database. Test which levers you can apply, particularly if investment funds for donor acquisition activities are hard to come by. Aim to improve your retention rates and increase your average gift then work on getting more donors.

You can see what a marked impact these levers can have on your fundraising income. Asking people for money is important. It is just as important to motivate them to continue to give year after year. It's about retaining those donors who were hard to attract in the first place.

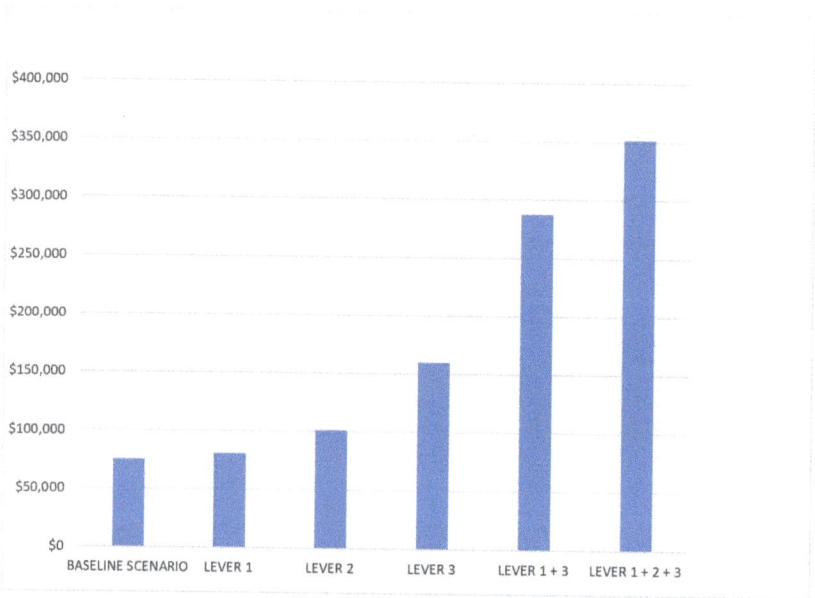

Graph 7: Total Money Raised $

In this chart we see how each lever, whether separately or in combination, performs in terms of income.

Consider which levers you will utilise and test how you can move your fundraising and your donors in the right direction.

Step 10: Fundraising income and expenditure budget

As we discussed in Stage 1 under Resources (money), your budget has two key components: how much you want to raise (income) and how much you have to spend (expenditure). The aim is to spend less than you intend to raise to deliver a positive ROI.

Your budget should show:

- the total amount to be raised: the income target
- the total amount to be spent: the expenditure budget

- the breakdown: how much to spend / raise by channel / type of donor
- the net return. Your ROI. How much you will raise for every dollar spent.

10.1 Budget by type of donor

An example: Here is a completed table of how you can break down your budget by channel and by types of donors based on a gross target of $72,500—an income goal of $62,500 and an expenditure budget of $10,000 which we want to get back.

In the table, we have identified the type of donor to be targeted, what we expect to raise from each segment (broken down by average donation), and the expected number of donations we need to achieve our goal.

As noted, acquiring smaller donations often requires more investment than acquiring larger donations. This is because you need a higher number of small donations with a smaller average donation value to reach your goal, and to do that, you need to ask more potential donors for a donation.

In our example, we will spend $10,000 and we want to recoup this and achieve our income target.

Type of donor	Targeted amount	Average donation	Number of donations required	Expenditure budget	Net return	ROI
Individual donors (giving <$500)	$10,000	$40	250	$5,000	$5,000	100%
Individual donors (giving >$500)	$20,000	$1,000	20	$2,500	$17,500	700%
Corporations	$2,500	$500	5	$1,000	$1,500	150%
Trusts and foundations	$40,000	$4,000	10	$1,500	$38,500	2,633%
Totals	$72,500		285	$10,000	$62,500	

10.2 Budget by marketing channel

Once you have determined how much you will spend on each target audience category or segment, you can decide how much you will need to spend on each channel. Using the previous example, the channel expenditure budget will look like this:

Type of donor	Expenditure budget	Fundraising channel
Individual donors (giving <$500)	$5,000	• acquisition direct mail pack • updated donation page on website
Individual donors (giving >$500)	$2,500	• personalised brochure • personal visits
Corporations	$1,000	• corporate brochure • leave behind brochure • personal visits
Trusts and foundations	$1,500	• grant research • written project descriptions • grant application assistance
Totals	$10,000	

Now you have decided on the cost of engaging with each segment of your target audiences and the channels you will use.

ACTION: Begin filling out the following template to identify who you will target and with which fundraising or marketing channels. At this point, you can be specific about how many of each segment you will target with which channels. You know how much you have to spend and how much you want to generate.

Target audience	Number of prospects targeted	Email	Telemarketing	Direct mail	TV / radio	Social media	Website	Face to face
Current donors (donated <$1,000 in the last 12 months)								
Prospective donors (never donated)								
Past donors (donated <$1,000 over 12 months ago)								
Trusts and foundations (never applied to before)								
Trusts and foundations (unsuccessfully applied)								
Trusts and foundations (successfully applied)								
Major donors (donated >$1,000 ever)								

Target audience	Number of prospects targeted	Email	Telemarketing	Direct mail	TV / radio	Social media	Website	Face to face
Major donors (never donated)								
Corporate sponsorship								

10.3 Determine your net return

You can see from the results that if your targeted amount is $72,500, you will need:

- 250 donations from individuals giving less than $500
- a total of 250 gifts.

Overall, you will raise $72,500 as this covers the cost of your $10,000 investment and gives a net return of $62,500.

In your strategy, you may not want or need to target all types of prospective donors or use all fundraising channels. Just fill in the details for the ones that apply to you. Now you have a map of how you are going to raise your funds.

SUMMARY

You can now implement your strategy using the elements of your written fundraising strategy:

- Your unique selling proposition.
- SMART goals.

- Determining your target audience/s.
- Fundraising income and expenditure budgets.

It's the moment for which you have been planning. You are ready to start implementing your strategy.

Stage 3

Implement your fundraising strategy

'The path to success is to take massive, determined actions.'

—Tony Robbins

IMPLEMENT YOUR FUNDRAISING STRATEGY

You have researched and you have planned. Now is the time to implement your strategy.

In Stage 3, we will look at what you will do to implement your fundraising strategy: the type of donor you will target, how you will target them and the fundraising and marketing channels you will use. This is where all your previous planning comes into action. The more detail you can put here, the better.

4-STAGE FUNDRAISING STRATEGY		
STEP	DESCRIPTION	YOUR PROGRESS
Stage 3: Implement your fundraising strategy		
11	Attract donors' attention: the AIDA Principle	
12	Determine marketing and fundraising channels	
	12.1 Direct response marketing vs mass marketing	
	12.2 Direct marketing appeals or campaign structure	
	12.3 Digital fundraising	
	12.4 Channel integration	
13	The Value/Effort matrix	
14	Create targeted fundraising plans	
	14.1 Structured campaigns and fundraising appeals	
	14.2 Developing a bequests, gifts in wills or legacies plan	
	14.3 Grants (applications to trusts and foundations)	
	14.4 Corporate sponsorship	
	14.5 Events	
	14.6 Major gift and capital fundraising campaigns	

4-STAGE FUNDRAISING STRATEGY		
STEP	**DESCRIPTION**	**YOUR PROGRESS**
15	Doing it all	
	15.1 Using outside suppliers	
	15.2 A campaign brief	
	15.3 The implementation calendar	
	15.4 Test. Test. Test.	
16	Caring for donor data	
	16.1 Donor financial data	
	16.2 Prospect data	
	16.3 Donor privacy and data protection	

Step 11: Attract donors' attention: the AIDA Principle

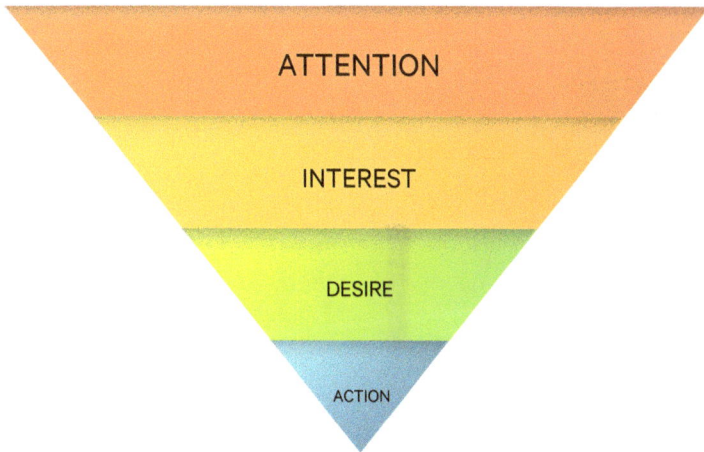

As discussed, fundraising is a component of marketing. In order to attract prospective donors, you will put your cause to them in a way that will attract their attention (remember, getting a donor's attention is essential if they are to donate) and then ask for a donation (the second most important requirement). In marketing, this is called the AIDA Principle. AIDA stands for Attention, Interest, Desire, Action.

Attention

Before anyone can donate to you, they need to know you exist. How will you get their attention? It starts, as discussed, by identifying who you want to target. Whose attention do you want to attract? If you are clear about your target audience, you can determine which channels and tools to use to get their attention.

Interest

To get their attention, they need to care about your cause. If the people you are targeting are not interested in your cause, they won't donate. You need to work out what will motivate them to act. You need to have thought about who you are targeting and their interests. What issues have they responded to before? Have they filled in a survey or responded to a newsletter? Focus on what is of interest to your prospects.

Desire

How can you create a desire for your target audience to act now? If your situation is time bound, for example, an emergency appeal, you could motivate them through a sense of urgency. Images of the devastation of the Australian bushfires motivated millions of people around the world to take action and donate to those who lost their homes—animal and human. Here's where you consider the acronym, WIIFM: What's in it for me? What's in it for the donor to support your cause? Maybe they want a sense of fulfilment or perhaps they feel outraged by a particular situation like the loss of habitat for a threatened species. Find a way to tap into their desire.

Action

What do you want them to do? You would be surprised at the number of fundraising appeals I have seen where there is no clear call to action. How do donors take action? Give them a phone number, a URL, an email address or a link to click. Whatever you do, choose one clear call to action and make it easy. Use all the elements above to make it obvious that they need to take action today.

Always provide a response mechanism

Whichever approach you choose, remember the golden rule: *always give your audience a direct, clear means of response*. This means giving them one or more of the following:

- A coupon to complete (for a letter or leaflet).
- A telephone number to call.
- An email address / link to click on.
- A website URL / link to click on.
- A link to a resource (a brochure, a video) to download.
- A link to a payment form to complete.
- A PayPal link.
- A 'leave behind': a brochure or flyer with your contact details that you leave with someone you've met in person.

With a response mechanism, you can measure and track responses to your activities, and you can work out strategies to improve your responses. Without a response mechanism, you can only hope that someone saw your message as you'll have no way of accurately measuring results.

As the AIDA diagram suggests, you will have a smaller number of people who act compared with those who notice you. Regardless of the size of the donation you want to attract, you will need to talk with more than one person to get a donation. To get the best conversion rate (the percentage of prospects you turn into donors), you will want to talk to those who are most likely to give you a donation.

Step 12: Determine marketing and fundraising channels

Earlier, you determined how many contacts you have in each category (prospect, donor or lapsed donor) by segmenting your donors and prospects. For each segment, you can create individual communications plans. You may want to communicate with each segment (category) in a different way. For example, you may want to email prospects and telephone current donors or a combination of both. By thinking through how you will contact each segment, you will clarify how you will use your resources (tools, people, time and money).

The main purpose of your implementation plan is to clarify how you will make the best use of the resources you have to realise your goals by deciding which marketing and contact channels you will use in your fundraising strategy.

The channels you choose will reflect the following:

- The key focus of your strategy (your objectives and goals).
- The audience you are trying to reach.
- The resources / budget you have available.
- How quickly you want to raise the funds.
- The size of your current prospect / donor base (how many people you have on your database).
- The size of the gift you are trying to attract.

The key focus of your strategy (your objectives and goals)

This is where you look to your strategic approach to support whether you use just one channel (for example, face to face) or multiple channels (for example, direct mail, website, email and telemarketing). It is important to be specific here and to think through which channels will best suit the segments you identified earlier.

The audience you are trying to reach

It is worth remembering that most donations come from individuals (directly or through a vehicle like a PAF or foundation) rather than companies or corporations. However, your strategy may be to attract sponsorship as a key priority. Remember, your strategy should reflect the types of contributors you are trying to attract.

The resources / budget you have available

If you have little money to invest in fundraising, you will not choose an expensive channel like television to promote your cause. If you know your total budget, you can break this down by the channels you want to use and see if it is viable to spread your budget across multiple channels or choose one or two to give you better bang for your buck.

Another example could be that you have a desire to telephone all donors who made gifts of over $1,000 in the last year but you don't have many of their telephone numbers. Before you give up on the idea, think through whether you can obtain their phone numbers. If not, how else can you contact them? This is the point of being specific; it forces you to think through your engagement or contact strategy.

How quickly you want to raise the funds

As discussed, some donations take much longer to acquire than others. If you have time and lots of past donors who really support your work, you could invest in a bequest or legacy strategy. Remember, bequests can take more than five years to arrive. If you need funds more quickly (and who doesn't?) then you will need to consider which channels will bring you a quicker return. It is worth remembering that small donations can be quicker to attract but you need a lot of them and it can be expensive to attract a lot of small donors to your cause.

The size of your current prospect / donor base (how many people you have on your database)

If you have a big donor database you can market to them directly via telephone, mail, email or even SMS. You will want to encourage current donors to give more than once and perhaps convert them to major donors or bequests. If you have few or no current donors, you will need to focus on acquisition. This means acquiring new donors to your cause and choosing the most appropriate channels to reach them.

The size of the gift you are trying to attract

Big gifts require personal donor attention; small gifts require mass marketing to lots of potential donors. If, for example, you are going to focus on attracting high net worth donors, you will want to invest in people who can build relationships and materials they can share with donors to encourage their interest. Tailor your marketing channels to the type of donor you are trying to attract.

12.1 Direct response marketing vs mass marketing

Once you have decided who you want to raise money from, you can narrow down how to reach them. This means deciding which media or channels you will use to promote your cause and ask for money. Broadly, there are two ways you can contact prospective customers or donors. Direct marketing is one-to-one and mass marketing is one-to-many. The bigger the gift, the more likely you will use a one-to-one approach.

The channels we will consider are:

Direct response marketing	Mass marketing
A targeted approach to selected specific groups of **identifiable** individuals with tailored, relevant messages.	A mass market approach to audience segment groups of **unidentifiable** individuals with relevant messages.
direct mail	television / radio
telemarketing	billboards
email (if they are targeted to individuals)	print
socials (if they are targeted to individuals)	digital advertising
face-to-face engagement	socials (if they are broadcast to the world)

Direct response marketing

Most fundraising channels require a response from a specific contact. This means the channels we will mostly use are direct marketing or direct response marketing channels.

This approach takes a targeted approach by selecting specific groups of **identifiable** individuals to approach with tailored messages. You consider what you want to say or what you want to deliver to each segment. You will know, up-front, who is likely to engage with you because you can see who responded to your communications—

95

you targeted specific individuals so you can precisely measure your response rate.

Direct marketing or direct response marketing involves a one-to-one approach and could include the following:

- Making a telephone call (telemarketing or telefundraising).
- Sending a personalised letter or email (direct mail or email marketing).
- Sending a personalised message (SMS).
- Visiting someone in person (face to face).

With direct marketing, you know who you are targeting. Whatever channel you use, it will always have a response mechanism: a means for the person to respond to your communication.

Direct mail

In a world where everything is digital, there is an entire generation that has grown up never having received a personal letter. Is there still room in the marketing world for direct mail? Well, yes. A high proportion of young Canadians, for example, are 'giving' via direct mail. They are proving to be more loyal donors than those giving by other channels.[14] In fact, in 2019, the research showed that revenue from direct mail increased from the previous year by more than 5%.

The donorCentrics® Index of Direct Marketing Fundraising in the United States looked at revenue from direct marketing for 61 organisations (of which direct mail was the primary tool) and reported that revenue per donor increased by 4.5% in 2019 with a greater percentage of organisations showing an increase in revenue compared with 2018.[15]

It's even more interesting that the median growth rate using direct marketing channels for the past ten years was 48.6%. However, a less positive trend is the decline in the number of people donating despite disasters and election-related increases. Overall donor numbers have declined over the ten-year period by 12.2%. This long-term decline relates in part to the types of donors being targeted by charities with a smaller number of HNWI giving larger gifts as well as changes in tax laws and the instruments donors use for giving. It probably also reflects a lack of attention by organisations on donor retention and stewardship, focusing instead on acquisition. So make sure you show your donors lots of love.

12.2 Direct marketing appeals or campaign structure

We talked before about direct response marketing and how important it is to have a response mechanism on all of your material. A good direct marketing campaign follows a structure:

- **The brief:** Write a tight brief even if you are writing all the material yourself. Nothing stimulates ideas like a strong brief. This means writing down what you want from the direct mail campaign (a direct mail plan) in a document that you can share with your staff, volunteers and / or suppliers.

- **Target audience:** Know to whom you are writing and why. Be clear who you are targeting.

- **Copy:** This is the text of your communications. It is the letter you will send to your target audience. What is the offer?

- **Design:** This is the layout and structure of your communications. How does it look? What images are included? How many pages does it contain? How many different elements are there? Are you using colour or is it all black and white?

- **Paper:** Will you use recycled paper? Gloss paper? Will it be Australian or purchased from overseas?

- **Envelopes:** These are your outside and return envelopes. You will need to put your letter in an outer envelope (with perhaps a promotional message on the outside) and a reply-paid envelope if you are using a coupon or other printed response mechanism so that your donor can return it to you.

- **Response mechanism:** For example, mail, telephone, email address, website URL or coupon. You must give your prospective donor a **measurable** way of replying to your communication. If you don't, you won't generate responses. Or if you send your donors to a generic website page, how will you know your mailing generated that response? You must provide a response mechanism you can track. When you receive it, you need to know the response was because of the mail pack.

- **Cause:** For what are you trying to get support? This is where your Case for Support comes in and all the research you did as to why anyone should donate to you. It must be motivational and inspiring. Go back and consider the AIDA principle. Get attention, encourage desire and inspire action.

- **Unique selling proposition:** Why should they support you? What is the one thing that makes you important? What makes you different from other non-profits? Why will you deliver a better result?

- **Testing:** Test your communication, your audience and your messaging. Before you action a mail out to your entire mailing list, test your mailing with a segment of your audience.

- **Follow up:** Don't leave your audience in limbo. Research says that the best time to ask for a donation is just after you've received one. Talk with your donor. Follow up by phone, email or mail.

- **Integration with other channels:** You can integrate your direct mail with your telemarketing, mail, online and other channels. It takes time, effort and planning but it is a way to ensure you don't waste marketing and fundraising actions.

Here are some considerations about direct response marketing thanks to advertising maverick Sir David Ogilvy:[16]

- **You know more about the results from direct response marketing than you do from general advertising campaigns.** General advertising campaigns often do not have a response mechanism. Your response mechanisms give you data on your results.

- **Long copy sells more than short copy.** It may seem counterintuitive but a long, well-crafted direct marketing letter with two or three pages will often outperform a short letter. This is likely because you have the space to *really* share your story with your prospective donor—this cannot be done in a short letter. Also, a short letter can feel impersonal. Consider a well-written two- to three-page letter, but only include what will attract interest, inspire desire and create action—a donation.

- **Headline and copy about the product and its benefits sell more.** Headlines, whether on an outer envelope or at the top of your letter (or advertisement), will 'pull' better (attract more interest) if they are about the product (or cause) and the benefits of it. Fluffy headlines that tell the reader little about the product or why they should care about it tend to have less impact.

- **It's not being creative or entertaining.** Your direct marketing is not a place to show off. You are trying to attract donations, not impress potential donors with your witticisms, puns or general cleverness. You are building relationships and you must respect your reader's intelligence.

Mass marketing

Mass marketing includes any activity where you push out your message to a wider audience. But you are not targeting specific individuals; you are targeting a mass audience even if you have segmented that audience. You won't know specifically who is likely to respond because you won't know who has received your message. You can provide response mechanisms for these audiences to respond to you, for example, a phone number or a URL. However, this is a scattergun approach.

Mass marketing could include the following activities:

- Putting a commercial on television or radio.
- Putting an advertisement in a newspaper or magazine.
- Putting up a poster: a billboard or transit media (a poster at a bus or tram stop).
- Running online banner ads.
- Standing outside a railway station approaching passers-by (face-to-face fundraising).

Why all this matters

The more you know about those with whom you are communicating and those who may respond to your messages, the better you will know where to invest your limited fundraising dollars and predict how much you are likely to raise from your audiences (and the better you can target future campaigns).

The more people with whom you try to connect, the more it will cost. The cheapest direct mail pack will cost you $2.00 to create and mail. This doesn't include the cost of acquiring the recipient's address, so choose wisely.

Your choice of channel will depend on who you want to reach and what information you have about them, for example, if you have their mailing address you can send them a direct letter. It will also depend on how quickly you need the funds.

Direct response marketing	Mass marketing
Send an email appeal to 5,000 prospects you have already identified. 25% open the email (1,250). 10% of those prospects (125) donate an average gift of $30 (Total $3,750).	Show a TV commercial on a commercial network. Target potential audiences at certain times of the day. With no response mechanism, you have no idea who has seen your ad or if it has been effective. The only way you can judge this is if your donations rise during the period you are running the ad. But you can't be sure the ad attracted the donations. If you included a response mechanism, a percentage of the estimated audience could visit a URL you promoted on the TV commercial. A smaller percentage will donate.
When you know who you will communicate with, you can estimate: • how many will give • who will give • how much they will give. You can also forecast your income and you can repeatedly communicate with everyone you have on your prospect list.	In this case, you can communicate only with those who visited the website if they gave you their contact details. Otherwise, you can communicate only with those who donated. To reach the broader audience again, you need to show the ad again.

12.3 Digital fundraising

Digital fundraising has many names: email marketing, online fundraising and crowdfunding. It is a rapidly growing area of fundraising but surprisingly it has yet to surpass all of the more traditional methods like direct mail or face-to-face fundraising in producing results. For example, no one has yet figured out how to convince HNWI donors to give big gifts online without cultivating them and talking with them in the real world.

When digital fundraising started it was mostly about blogs, websites, e-newsletters and outbound emails with simple technology. Now there are highly integrated models such as online giving days that utilise a combination of real-time giving and results online, and telemarketing and major gift offline cultivation to attract new donors in a short window of, say, 48 hours.

That said, digital fundraising is an essential part of your fundraising strategy if you use email, have a website or have donors with a smartphone. And that's pretty much everyone. But the essentials still hold true: to convert prospects to donors they need to know about your cause and be asked to donate. And to use digital fundraising as a channel within your fundraising strategy, you need goals and identification of the donors with whom you want to engage.

Forms of digital fundraising

New online platforms, applications (apps) and tools appear every day.

And who would have thought that QR codes would make a comeback? Living with the COVID-19 epidemic meant we are using 'check in' technology by scanning QR codes on our smartphones. These are also being used for fundraising purposes.

Here are some of the various types of digital fundraising and some ways to use them to enhance and grow your fundraising results. These channels are developing so fast that I won't even try to capture all the digital ways you could fundraise.

Websites

Your website is one of the first places donors will look to check out who you are and what you will do with their donation. Your website should have an easy to find and operate donation form that you can customise for different levels of donations with opportunities to answer questions from visitors. Your website donations page should also provide motivational and useful information to encourage donations.

There are many ways to track where donors are coming from by using website and search engine optimisation tools. You can also guide visitors by applying navigation tools to help them find what they are looking for. The details on optimising your website are outside the scope of this book but it is becoming essential to allow for better targeting, tracking and conversion of prospects to donors.

You need to make it easy for donors to give. You would be surprised how difficult it can be for donors to figure out how or why to donate via your website or in response to an email. The NextAfter Institute recently reviewed online giving and email communications by 630 organisations in nine countries. It was found that donation pages needed to provide much more compelling reasons to encourage donors to give. As evidence, it found that three out of ten organisations used no text at all on their donation page to explain why donors should give and just four in ten organisations provided more than four sentences to clarify why a donation is needed and how it would be used.

To not use your donation pages to motivate donors is a waste of resources. If you have spent time and money to get people to that page, give them that final motivation to donate. You don't want donors 'abandoning their shopping cart' without making a transaction. Use images and text on your donation page (and your website generally) to motivate donors to give.

Smartphones and SMS / texting

Smartphones are becoming ubiquitous and it's therefore mandatory that your website or donation page should be optimised to appear and operate effectively on these devices. New apps are being developed regularly to encourage donations via smartphones.

When SMS / text messages first appeared, many charities tried to use them for fundraising purposes. In a lot of cases it backfired because prospective donors saw it as intrusive spam as they didn't have a relationship with the charities. Now charities are using SMS more strategically—after getting opt-ins (permission)—to thank donors or notify them of updates on their programs. It is a cheap way to quickly connect with donors and is used more effectively in recent times in conjunction with other channels as a useful communications tool.

Email and email newsletters

Email is used so extensively that it is hard for charities to cut through with fundraising communications; however, it is so important to get this right. Donors want to hear how donations are being spent and the impact they are making. Email should be used in conjunction with other channels (direct mail or telemarketing) and not just when someone signs up to a newsletter or visits your website.

Newsletters are often used as a way to attract new prospective donors. The NextAfter research shows that you need to give people a good reason to sign up to your email newsletter as it was found that only one out of four organisations (25%) globally gave a 'strong' reason for someone to sign up for email. Less than half the time (45%), it wasn't clear why someone should sign up or what they would receive from the organisation if they did sign up. So, if you think about it, if people don't know what they are going to receive from you, they may not open your emails or care very much what you send them.

Email considerations:

- Ensure the email is sent from a real person. Emails are opened more often if they come from a person not a company email address. For example, send your email from 'Sally Smith' rather than 'ABC Company'.

- Don't put all your potential donors' email addresses in the BCC line and hope they'll be happy with that. They won't. Ensure they get a personalised email as sending an email like this can look like spam and contravene some spam laws.

- Personalise the email with the donor's name. No one likes to receive a communication with a salutation that reads 'Dear Sir or Madam' or worse 'Dear Donor' as the opening line. Personalise it.

- Use stories, images and videos to bring your cause and vision to life.

- Use dynamic links to take donors to customised donation pages where they can donate and share more of their information with you, for example, their postcode, or take another action like signing a petition. You may even be able to upgrade them from a one-off donation to a regular monthly donation.

Crowdfunding

Crowdfunding is mass fundraising usually done online via a fundraising platform. Crowdfunding websites include GoFundMe, Kickstarter, Upwork and MyCause. More are appearing every day.

Each donor contributes an amount to help the beneficiary achieve a pre-determined goal. In some cases, donors receive rewards for gifting higher amounts. The donation is often only finalised if the beneficiary reaches their targeted goal. What is unusual about crowdfunding is that the beneficiary could be an individual, a company or a group. It does not need to be a charity or even have a charitable focus.

There are several versions of crowdfunding from helping to raise money for charities through raising money to launch new products, companies or even to get a film off the ground.

Crowdfunding considerations:

- Most platforms charge a fee. Ensure you understand what the fees are before you set out.
- Friends and family will make up a big part of your funding network. Ensure you are happy to ask everyone you know to contribute and to get their friends involved.
- Have a goal. Figure out how much you want to raise and how much you can invest in rewards and incentives. However, there is no guarantee that you'll reach your funding goal in the set time.
- Develop rewards and incentives. Give rewards to those who are willing to contribute higher amounts.
- Look at other similar listings and compare whether you can invest the time and energy to do something similar.

- Thank and communicate with everyone regularly. You need to reach your goal in order for the donations to be received.

- It's an opportunity to directly interact with your customers (who are also your investors or donors) and see donations happen in real time.

- It's a low commitment and risk (if you don't reach your goal, you don't have to commit and you don't usually pay any fees).

- If you do reach your goal, you must ensure you provide rewards to your backers to encourage donations.

- A big part of the success of crowdfunding is that the person raising the money can be trusted to deliver on their promises. Remember you are entering into an agreement to deliver the product, service or event to your supporters if you reach your goal.

- You will need to stand out from the competition so it still helps to have a plan in place and not rely on crowdfunding as a one-hit wonder.

Peer to Peer (P2P) fundraising

Peer to peer (P2P) fundraising is similar to crowdfunding. It means using *your* friends and networks and *your* current donors to help raise the funds you need by involving *their* friends and networks. You are trying to leverage one donor's interest with one or more of their friends, and each gets involved and spreads the message wider and wider. Some P2P is done via events or because an idea has gone 'viral'. Who doesn't remember the 'Ice Bucket Challenge'? This P2P campaign took the world by storm and helped raise over US$100 million for ALS or Lou Gehrig's disease—a progressive nervous system disease. The campaign enabled the ALS Association to increase its annual research funding by 187%. In some cases, the 'challenge' was taken up by celebrities who didn't know much about the cause but were happy to spread the word and raise money.

Another wildly successful P2P example is Movember. This is a great idea as it can be hard to encourage men to actively fundraise and even harder to get them to talk about men's mental health. Who knew that encouraging men to grow moustaches and then ask their friends and family to sponsor them would do the job?! Since its launch, Movember has become a global phenomenon with a community of Mo Bros (and now Mo Sisters) funding hundreds of men's health projects around the world. It's one of my favourite campaigns and causes.

P2P fundraising considerations:

- Who do you want to motivate and what action should they take? You need a clear idea of who you want to target and what you want them to do.

- It must be easy to communicate and understand. If it's too hard to understand, people won't 'get it' and will switch off.

- The action should probably be fun. If it's too serious, that may be a turn-off. Though there are always exceptions. The P2P campaign the 'World's Greatest Shave', where people are asked to shave off their hair to raise funds for people affected by cancer, is a pretty serious ask—but lots of people do it.

- It should be something that almost everyone can do. If it's too hard or too expensive, it's unlikely to take off.

- You need a plan and investment to provide tools to your audience to share with their networks.

- You need commitment to communicate widely and motivate participants to stay the course.

- You need a deadline. Movember is in November which helps people remember it and understand that it's for a specific period. I've just finished Dry July (a P2P where you are sponsored by your friends and family to stop drinking alcohol for a month to raise money for your chosen charity). It's just for one month and on August 1st you can open the wine bottle again.

- It helps if you have a ready-made audience like a donor or membership base to kick things off.

- Use social media and integrate with your other fundraising channels. Maximise all your donor and community touch points to spread the message.

Social media

Social media is another big part of many people's lives and, therefore, has become an important element of any fundraising strategy. Social media fundraising is a book all of its own so we will just scratch the surface here. Suffice it to say, all of your fundraising channels can benefit from integration with your social media activities and vice versa.

The most well-known platforms include Facebook, TikTok, Instagram, Twitter, WeChat and YouTube. There are probably hundreds if not thousands more tailoring to wide or niche markets. All offer opportunities to connect and communicate with a global audience of supporters, buyers, members and donors.

With social media, there is a huge emphasis on posting photos and videos. Indeed, it was this obsession that helped make the Ice Bucket Challenge so successful. We loved watching celebrities pour freezing water over their heads. It's hard to imagine how this could ever have worked so successfully without social media.

If your contact loves the cause and the right motivation pops up in front of them while they are scrolling through Facebook, you will get that donor to make a long-term commitment to support you. The challenge then is to continue to build on that relationship with those donors and encourage them to take more actions with you and possibly get their friends involved as well.

Social media considerations:

- Social media can be a wonderful extension of your brand, helping to reach parts of the market that would otherwise be unreachable.

- It can be highly measurable. You know through analytics, targeting, measurement and optimisation how much you are spending on whom and for what outcomes. This is one of its greatest assets: measurability and accountability.

- You can automate. Once you have figured out your strategy through testing and no small amount of trial and error, you can use what you've learned to automate your systems to deliver leads, donors or event participants—another great advantage of the digital world.

- It's time consuming (and a bit addictive). While social media offers endless opportunities, it can be time consuming. It helps if you have someone (a paid staff member or a volunteer) who can help manage your 'socials'.

- It makes giving easy—it's what we want for all our donors.

- You can set up recurring donations and have donors stay with you for years.

- Make it a part of your broader fundraising strategy. Digital fundraising is important and is a part of an organisation's overall fundraising strategy.

- It is not free. While it may not cost much to send an email or even 1,000 emails, there are costs to set up and manage the technology and data. You will need an expenditure budget and an income target.

- You need measurable goals. Figure out what you want to achieve with your digital fundraising, for example, the number of new email newsletter signups, Facebook supporters and first-time donors.
- You should target your audience. Which segments of your community, donors or prospective donors will you target using digital fundraising?

12.4 Channel integration

When I worked for Ogilvy & Mather Direct in their SoHo office in London (my first real advertising agency job), I heard about something called 'orchestration'. It was a term to describe what we now know as 'integration'. This is where marketeers bring together all of their marketing and fundraising activities into one symphonic strategy. Everything works with everything else to bring about the results.

Integration has always resonated with me because when you create a strategy you want the activities within that strategy to work well with each other. Here's an example: Imagine you want to include direct mail, telemarketing and email marketing in your fundraising strategy. You could write separate plans for each channel and implement them. Or you could consider how these channels could work together to improve results (while keeping the donor at the centre of the strategy).

A single donor may receive one or more of these communications: a phone call, an email or a direct mail pack. Imagine what would happen if a donor received them all? Would the communications interrelate? Would they appear to come from the same organisation? Does anything not feel right? It's not just a matter of having the same branding. Each message in each channel should build on or at least complement the next. So you should think about the content (the message, the graphics, the words) as well as the order in which the donor receives the message. Should the phone call, the email or the letter come first?

Your strategy may have a natural flow. You may decide to write to your donors then follow up with a phone call to those who didn't respond to the letter and then send a thank-you email. This is a simple example of integration: using different channels and methods to bring about a better result. The opposite is when you send out separate emails, letters and phone calls and don't think about who is receiving them and what they will think and what action they will take when they get them. Whenever possible, integrate your activities to maximise results.

Step 13: The Value/Effort matrix

Once you have worked out who to target, how do you decide which channels and activities to use in order to get your potential donors' attention? There are a variety of methods to attract donors. Begin with the Value/Effort matrix. The aim is to implement the activities that give you the best value ROI for your effort (fundraising activities).

I first came across this matrix when I was director of the Zoos Victoria Foundation. It has proved very useful in a range of situations to help determine where to place energies and resources (time, money, people and tools).

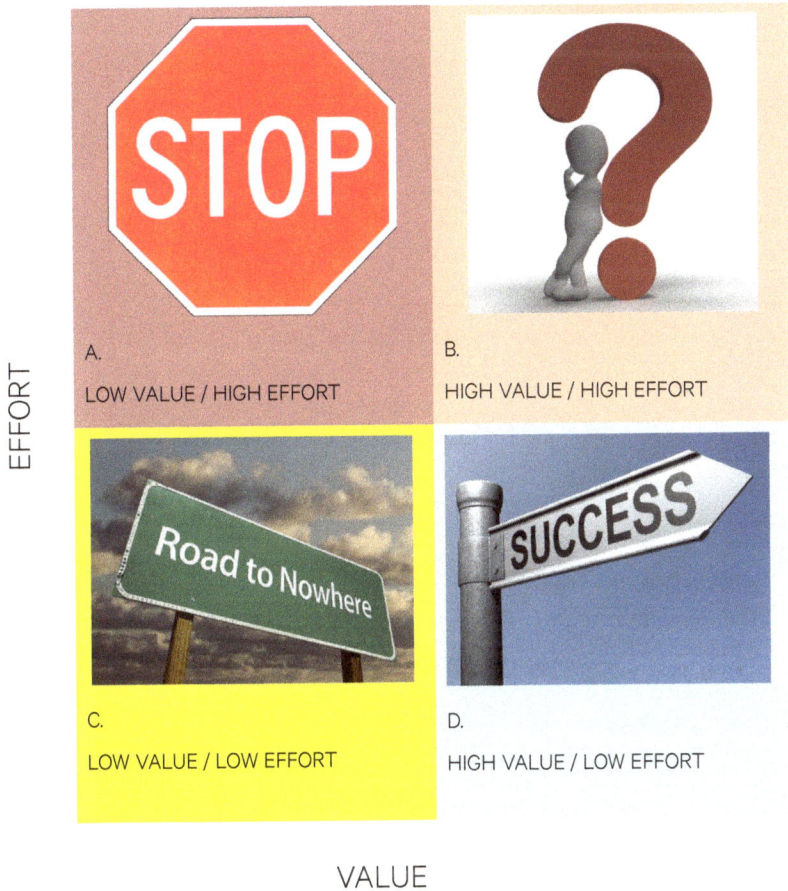

A.	B.
LOW VALUE / HIGH EFFORT	HIGH VALUE / HIGH EFFORT
C.	D.
LOW VALUE / LOW EFFORT	HIGH VALUE / LOW EFFORT

EFFORT

VALUE

The four boxes illustrate how every activity requires a degree of effort to deliver a measure of value.

- Effort equates to the amount of time, money or resources you need to invest.
- Value equates to the amount of money or benefit you gain from the activity.
- Your aim is to get the most value from the least effort (Quadrant D).

A Low value, high effort	**B** High value, high effort
The least desirable activities deliver the least value for the most effort. If you are putting in a lot of effort for little value in return, you should stop or seriously re-engineer those activities. Example: You are running an annual event that takes considerable amounts of time and resources. The event costs $100,000 to run and you only raise $120,000.	You are getting good results but you are investing a lot of effort to get those results. Look at how to reduce the amount of effort you are putting in to get the same or similar results. You want to transition items in Quadrant B to Quadrant D. Example: You are implementing an end of financial year appeal that generates a 20% ROI but with a big up-front cash cost.
C Low value, low effort	**D** High value, low effort
You have to wonder why you would bother with these activities as they are pretty much a waste of time and resources, and they are a distraction. These are sometimes the 'easy' things to do but why bother if they don't generate much income? Example: You are running a sausage sizzle outside your local hardware store. You raise $100 each time.	This is the sweet spot. It is where you get the most for less. It is where you extract as much value (dollars) in exchange for the least amount of investment in money, time and resources. Example: You are applying for targeted grants using one staff member and a volunteer. You achieve $250,000 per year, which gives an ROI of 75%.

ACTION

1. Take out a piece of paper or open a new Word document on your computer.

2. Draw four squares like the diagram above.

3. Fill in each box describing all of the activities you are doing or planning to do. Do this quickly. Instinctively allocate each activity to the most appropriate box.

4. What do you see? How many of your activities fit in box D and how many fit in box C?

If you have too many activities in the 'high effort' or 'low value' boxes, now is the time to reconsider your strategy. For example, if 50% of your annual target comes from a very high effort event, how could you reduce the investment or increase the income?

Now that you have a plan articulating what you want to achieve and how you will go about achieving it, you can start implementing it.

Step 14: Create targeted fundraising plans

Within your fundraising strategy, you will want to create targeted fundraising plans that integrate with one another for particular areas like:

- structured campaigns and fundraising appeals

  - major gift fundraising campaigns
  - capital campaigns and feasibility studies
  - annual fundraising appeals

- gifts in wills (legacies or bequests)
- grants (applications to trusts and foundations)
- corporate sponsorship
- events.

14.1 Structured campaigns and fundraising appeals

As well as major gift (high net worth) donations and fundraising approaches, organisations will usually conduct regular fundraising appeals to attract smaller individual donations.

These appeals are regular, timed communications (letters, emails, phone calls) that you present to your prospective donors asking them to donate to support your work.

These appeals can be seasonal, time bound or campaign-related.

An example of a **seasonal** campaign is Christmas, Easter, Mother's Day, Hanukkah or another 'time of year' opportunity to link your cause to people's sense of goodwill and willingness to donate. In order for your donors to donate at such a time, the connection needs to make sense. For example, if yours is a secular organisation, you may want to leverage the goodwill at Christmas but call your appeal an 'end of year' campaign rather than a Christmas campaign.

A **time bound** appeal means that the donor needs to act before 'time runs out'. So an 'End of Financial Year' or 'End of Calendar Year' appeal will require the donor to act before a deadline. In the case of end of financial year, in Australia, the donor can get a tax deduction in the same financial year they make the gift if they donate before June 30th. This is a very popular time bound tactic for many charities and the time of year when they achieve their best appeal results.

If you work in a sector that regularly responds to humanitarian emergencies, for example, floods, famine, contagion and bushfires, you will have extremely time bound appeals. By their nature, emergency appeals require short deadlines and quick action. These deadlines are used to maximise support for your emergency response work before the calamity is out of the media headlines and to get the money to take immediate action.

A **campaign-related** appeal would connect with some other activity you have underway. If you are running an engagement activity, for example, a fun run or crowdfunding campaign, you may want to integrate a direct mail fundraising appeal into this activity so that you maximise your fundraising and donor engagement.

These structured fundraising appeals offer several benefits:

- Create a sense of urgency encouraging donors to 'give now'.
- Provide untied / unrestricted income. Your appeal can request unrestricted funds that you can apply to your chosen priorities.
- Identify potential major donors as you may receive larger than expected gifts from certain individuals who can be channelled into your major gift strategy.
- Provide donors with an apparent benefit from giving now, for example, a tax deduction in the year they have donated.
- Attract donations from new donors. Appeals are good vehicles for converting prospects to new donors.
- Be prepared well in advance and set to deliver at the appropriate time. For example, a direct marketing appeal where you are using direct mail and telemarketing can be planned and tested ready for when you want to make 'the ask'.
- Be effectively utilised across various channels (direct mail, telemarketing, face to face, email, SMS, crowdfunding) with related and consistent messaging to provide multiple contact points for your donor to engage with your cause.
- Be implemented multiple times each year. Some charities implement twelve appeals a year. Three is a good start: end of calendar year, end of financial year and one other. This way you will learn what works and can develop your fundraising appeal 'muscle'.

Structured campaigns and fundraising appeals considerations:

- Like any fundraising, appeals require prospective donors to whom you can send the appeal. So you will need a combination of known donors and prospective donors, as we have discussed, and their contact details.

- Perform a cost-benefit analysis prior to conducting an appeal. Determine how much you need to raise and, therefore, how much you can spend to deliver your goal. Like other forms of fundraising, you can test your appeal before you send it to your entire list.

- Seasonal or time bound appeals by their nature require you to be ready to take advantage of the deadline you are setting your donors. As an example, this means you cannot send out a Christmas appeal in January. So you need to be ready with your materials to send out well in advance of the deadline to give your donors time to respond (and January is either very much too soon or too late.)

- If you regularly face emergency-related conditions, help yourself by setting in place trusted advisers (mail houses, telemarketing agencies, media agencies, copywriters, graphic designers, marketing and fundraising consultants) who will help you quickly respond to the emergency without derailing your regular fundraising activities by pulling away essential internal resources. Create a triage plan that is put into action when a new emergency appeal is required.

- Beware calling every appeal an 'emergency'. Some charities have been criticised for suggesting in their materials that the need is 'urgent' and then holding on to donor funds that were given for the charity to take 'immediate action'. If you are not going to spend the funds quickly, make sure your donors know this before they donate. If you keep shouting 'emergency' and your donors don't believe you, they will stop giving.

Structured fundraising appeals are opportunities to connect your cause with the goodwill of the season, for donors to benefit from a time bound goal such as the end of financial year or to create a greater sense of urgency to encourage your donors to give right now.

Every appeal you conduct will provide vital information on how to improve on it next time. Use the recommendation ROI analysis to determine in advance what success looks like and measure your results against this. Then look at what you need to change to get a better result next time.

14.2 Developing a bequest, legacy or gifts in wills plan

Bequests are also known as gifts in wills or legacies. Developing a bequest plan requires time from committed, sensitive staff rather than a large fundraising budget. Implementation of a bequest plan does not require your organisation to have a tax deductibility status. This is a major benefit for many organisations.

Any bequest plan must, by its nature, take a long-term view. Your donor may decide to leave you a bequest long before you actually receive it. This can be many years, even decades, into the future. Work done today to cultivate bequest donors may perhaps only see a measurable financial result after the bequest staff member who engaged with the donor has left the organisation. However, this is not a reason to delay implementing a bequest strategy.

The aim of a bequest plan

The aim of a bequest plan is to encourage current or future donors to include your organisation in their will, preferably with an 'untied' donation where the organisation can decide how it will apply the donation to its future strategy.

To measure the success of your strategy, you will measure three lead and lag indicators. Lead indicators can forecast the future and lag indicators measure things after they happen.

Lead indicators

Bequest enquiries

These form part of your bequest pipeline. The more people who enquire about making a bequest, the more likely you are to attract confirmed bequests. Encouraging bequest enquiries should be a key part of your bequest strategy.

Confirmed bequests

Confirmed bequests give you an indication of what will happen to the future of your bequest program. Confirmed bequests are people who have told you they will include a donation to your organisation in their will. They may even tell you how much the bequest will be. Just knowing that you are in their will is all the information you need.

If you can measure the number of people who confirm they will leave your organisation a bequest (particularly if they put this confirmation in writing), you will have a good indication of how many people will leave you an actual bequest in the future. The more bequests you confirm (assuming the donor does not change their will), the more actual bequests you will receive. In some cases, a donor will advise whether they will leave a particular percentage of their estate or a specific amount to your organisation. Again, this information allows you to forecast future actual bequests.

As actual bequests can take many years to eventuate, measuring enquiries and confirmed bequests is a good indicator of how your work is progressing and whether you are making an impact on your donor base. You can use this information to report to management to show how the bequest strategy is progressing. This data can help support requests by the development team for further or continued investment in the bequest strategy.

Lag indicators

Actual bequests

Actual bequests are lag indicators. Actual bequests are the result of confirmed bequests. You will only receive actual bequests if you have asked for them while the donor is alive or the donor put you in their will without you asking. Actual bequests represent the financial contributions your organisation receives once a donor's will has passed through probate, i.e. the estate has been finalised.

Actual bequests can range from a token donation to the entirety of a donor's estate. Whatever the scope of the bequest, the final figure is not known until the estate has been valued, particularly when real estate or other valuable assets must be sold before bequests can be distributed.

Bequest considerations:

Once the results of your bequest activity start to make an impact (and you are receiving regular bequests each year), the organisation can begin to forecast future bequest income with a degree of accuracy. It is important, however, to continue your bequest strategy even when you have not seen any actual bequests. The time it takes for your first bequest to appear will depend on a few factors:

a. **The length of time your organisation has been in operation.** A new organisation is less likely to attract bequests compared to an organisation that has been around for many years. It takes time to show results and to build donor trust.

b. **Whether you have built a strong donor community.** If you have few donors, you must convert more of them into bequests and this can be difficult. As you build your donor community, the number of bequests you receive will increase as a percentage of your overall donations.

c. **The average age of your donor community.** While a will can be written at any age, most bequests are received from donors who have reached the age of 60 or older. Therefore, if the average age of people on your donor list is 33, you may have to wait a long time for your first actual bequest.

d. **Your willingness to ask.** Bequests are viewed as a delicate and sensitive subject—which they are. However, each of us must decide to whom we will leave our estate. Therefore, learn how to ask for a bequest. You will achieve more success in this area if you help your leadership team and development staff learn the skills to broach this subject with care and honesty. Most donors are happy to discuss their bequest plans with you if the subject is raised in an appropriate manner.

e. **Your allocation of resources.** While bequest strategies do not require a large financial investment, they do require a good CRM system to capture data, strong transparent processes and people to engage with potential bequests.

Wording

To encourage more donors to put your organisation in their will, you can provide them with sample wording to give to their legal adviser.

This wording can be displayed on your website and other promotional collateral. An example of sample wording is in the appendices.

Legal

With a few exceptions, staff within charities and other non-profit organisations are not legal experts. Therefore, always encourage your donors to seek independent professional advice before they change or set up their will. Encourage your donors to think of their family first and discuss any potential bequest to your organisation with other family members. In this way, bequest disagreements can be reduced to a minimum as other family members are made aware of their relative's wishes.

14.3 Grants (applications to trusts and foundations)

These are organised groups of individuals who have collectively decided to pool their funds and distribute their donations. They are non-profit organisations that keep funds 'in trust' for the benefit of the public. They will usually hold a corpus of funds and give away a percentage of these funds each year or when they choose. In the case of family foundations, they could be groups of family members or like-minded people who believe in a common cause or mission. They will provide funding for projects and programs. Private foundations are often created by individuals (perhaps by a bequest) and can have specific areas of interest. Community foundations can be set up by organisations or individuals and may service a particular geographic area or demographic group.

Trusts and foundations can have loose or stringent application procedures and often have formal acquittal requirements, i.e. you need to tell them how you have spent the funds they provided. While this can seem challenging, trusts and foundations are an excellent source of funds for many non-profit organisations.

Grants can range from $500 to multi-millions of dollars. Usually, trusts and foundations have rules around the types of organisations to which they can give. Foundations are usually governed by a board of trustees who help guide where funds should be allocated rather than one person making the decision about where to make the donation.

Grant applications

Grant applications need to be submitted in order to attract funds from trusts and foundations and involve a different fundraising approach compared with soliciting donations from individual donors. Why? Because you are not asking an individual for a gift; you are asking a committee or a board of a foundation.

What's the difference between a grant and a donation?

There are a few differences between a grant and a donation. A grant is usually structured giving from an organisation and a donation is more likely to come from an individual.

1. Often you will not meet the people from whom you are asking for the grant before you make the application.
2. Often a grant will require you to meet certain requirements or application criteria such as governance structure or DGR status to make an application.
3. Grantors will often ask you to 'acquit' the grant, i.e. provide a written report to tell them how you spent the grant.
4. Grants are often tied to specific projects about which you will need to advise on outcomes and outputs.

Grant considerations:

- Trusts and foundations will require you, most of the time, to complete a formal written application providing details of your organisation and how you will utilise the funds you are requesting. This can take hours or weeks depending on a) the size of the potential grant, b) the size of the project to be funded and c) the complexities of the funding entity. It is important that you collect as much of the information needed for the grant application before you try to complete it. And, before you start the application, ensure that your organisation qualifies to receive funds from the trust or foundation.

- When you are considering applying for a grant, read the trust and foundation guidelines, and confirm that your organisation complies and qualifies to get the funds. It is disheartening to go through the process only to fall at this first hurdle. Check if your organisation:

  - needs to be in a particular state or territory
  - needs to service a particular segment of the community (children, animals, etc.)
  - can show it has the capacity to acquit the grant within the time allowed
  - meets any other specific requirements of the grant application.

- Depending on the sophistication of the foundation, you can usually find the grant details on the organisation's website or in the grant application guidelines. Some smaller foundations and corporate foundations don't advertise their grant programs, which makes finding the guidelines tricky. But that is the joy and frustration of grant programs. It is as much about your capacity to find the grant opportunity as it is about how you complete a winning and compelling application.

- It is always worthwhile looking for grant opportunities. Not all non-profit organisations will make the effort or will cease the process at the point they find it's all 'a bit too hard'. So go the extra step and get prepared. You may well attract significant funding for your cause.

Government

Local, state and national government entities will provide grants to certain types of organisations. They usually have formal application processes and require a high degree of detail about how the funds will be spent. They also require a lot of reporting after the funds have been received by the charity. This book does not deal with government funding but it is recognised as a major source of funding for many organisations in the non-profit sector.

Grants can attract other donors

Grants can provide your organisation with a success story to share with potential donors, and success attracts success. Research has shown that government funding, when leveraged with philanthropic donors, will result in an increase in donations.[17] This 'crowding in' means that when donors hear you have had success with government or foundation funders, they gain confidence and want to be associated with that success. So use your successful grant applications to leverage more philanthropic support.

14.4 Corporate sponsorship

In my experience, more funding is available in a company's marketing department compared with its foundation or staff social club. These are sponsorship funds and are used to help increase the company's sales by leveraging external activities that offer them an increased positive profile and enhanced corporate kudos. These include sponsoring sporting events (think advertising at a rugby or football match), arts activities (like sponsoring major art exhibitions) or some non-profit organisations where association with the non-profit will help the company's brand— making it look good and likely to sell more products or services.

The top 200 companies or those listed on the stock exchange will likely have a formal corporate sponsorship or CSR strategy. Again, few publish them and often the requirements are opaque and subject to the whims of senior management or their own corporate goals. However, acquiring corporate sponsors is like acquiring major donors. Relationships count. If you can make good connections with individuals within corporations who will support your cause and promote you to the appropriate leadership in the marketing and sponsorship departments, you are more likely to gain support. And here the financial rewards can be significant. Once acquired, sponsorship agreements can be offered for one year, three years or even five years if the company sees value in the partnership.

Corporate sponsors require servicing. They expect a return on their investment, so when you acquire a corporate sponsor, consider that a percentage of the funds they give you will need to be utilised to service the relationship. The sponsor's senior leadership may expect to meet with your own high net worth donors, so you'll need to put on an event for them to attend. They may want to promote their brand to your supporters, so you'll need to consider where to put signage or branding. You may need to invest in new brochures and other marketing collateral so that their logo and support of your event can be advertised—in sponsorship, there is no such thing as a free lunch.

While each company is different, consider the following if you are intending to pursue corporate sponsorship agreements:

Consider:	Why?
Are you a national or state-based organisation?	Companies may only support organisations in their local area or those that have a national presence they can leverage.
Do you have a large supporter base?	If you have thousands of supporters, companies may be interested if they can leverage your supporter base to promote their products.
Do you have a strong marketing / promotional strategy?	Can you maximise the partnership? The benefit of a sponsorship is not just the funding but the charity's capacity to leverage and build its own brand through the partnership.
Do you have staff / volunteers who can service the relationship?	Corporate sponsors require servicing. This takes time and resources. You will need to make them feel loved and give them a measurable return on their investment. Unloved relationships end sooner—and usually not well.
What can you offer a potential sponsor that they would see as valuable?	What do you have that they want? If you are a sports club, perhaps you have an oval and team uniforms with signage possibilities? Perhaps you have a large database of supporters to whom the company could promote its products?
Do you have any existing individual relationships within corporations that you can leverage?	Corporate sponsorships often come through personal relationships. Who do you know who could help you?
Does your cause resonate with the company's corporate strategy or objectives?	If you are focused on indigenous health and the company isn't involved in any related services or doesn't operate in the same geographic areas, they may be unlikely to support you. Look at alignments and similarities. Where do your company interests intersect?

Consider:	Why?
Do you have any skeletons in your closet?	If you know of something in your history that may embarrass or put off a potential sponsor, don't hide it. Flush it out and consider doing something about it. Discuss it early in the negotiations to ensure it doesn't turn into a bigger issue later.

Corporate social responsibility

When a company has a formal strategy for engaging with the community by helping non-profit organisations deliver their services or by providing skilled volunteers, it is called a corporate social responsibility (CSR) strategy. As with corporate sponsorship, not all companies promote their strategies but the larger ones will and you'll find details on their websites.

Pro bono / In-kind support

Corporates may be more willing to support you with pro bono or in-kind (free) services or products than they are to provide you with cash. It is how you leverage this support that makes it useful. For example, legal firms may provide pro bono legal advice instead of offering funding. Supermarkets may offer free or discounted groceries you can sell or give to your constituency. In rare cases, car companies may offer a free car to use in a raffle in exchange for access to your supporters to promote their cars or book test drives.

The analysis you do before you accept or agree to pro bono or in-kind support is value versus effort. As we have seen above, some activities require lots of effort (work) to achieve very few dollars (value). If a company offers you a lot of free product but you have no way of using it or disposing of it for a profit or in a way that helps your cause, you may find yourself having to pay storage costs on items you didn't really want.

However, if you currently pay large amounts for accounting or legal services, the offer of pro bono advice from these types of providers may be welcome and may save you a considerable amount of expenditure that you can then invest in other areas of your organisation.

Consider value versus effort before you agree to these types of sponsorship agreements. Even with pro bono and in-kind support, companies may still want something in return. So think twice before you accept products instead of cash in a sponsorship agreement. Make sure it is something that is useful to you.

Sponsorship agreements

It is always good to have your sponsorship agreements written down so that each party knows what has been agreed. A handshake or verbal agreement is never sufficient. Why? Staff change and verbal agreements may not be honoured by the next manager. Anything verbal is also subject to 'misremembering' or just plain confusion over time. You thought you were getting one thing and the company thought it was giving another. Get it in writing. Confirmation emails between both parties can clarify what is going to happen. With larger organisations, a formal written agreement signed by both parties is usual practice.

Even (especially) if you have a fantastic relationship with the company, get your agreements in writing and get them signed by a manager in charge. Don't be concerned that the company will be offended if you ask for this—commercial agreements require clarity and are normally written down. They are not sponsoring your organisation out of love; they expect some kind of return in exchange for their financial investment. Get it written down and it will help both parties in 6- or 12-months' time when the memory of verbal agreements becomes blurry.

If the company will not provide you with anything in writing, you may want to consider how this relationship will travel over time. At the very least, write down your own version of how things will be done and your expectations and deliverables, and send this to the company. At least it is written down at your end.

14.5 Events

Types of events

Events can range from mass gatherings such as sponsored walks, bike rides or marathons targeting large numbers of individuals or team participants, to black-tie dinners targeting extremely HNWI at expensive ticket prices. Examples include:

- Sporting events (walks, marathons, cycle rides, footy matches, golf matches).
- Cultural events (ballet, opera, festivals, orations, musical theatre, exhibitions, fetes).
- Dinners and balls (black-tie dinners, dances, gala balls).
- Free or paid (could be free to enter but there are other charges on arrival or to participate).

Deciding which events are right for your purposes

Like any fundraising activity, you will need to consider what type of event is right for your organisation and you can do that by asking yourself some questions:

- Do I have enough people on my database or CRM system who might agree to attend an event?
- Does this type of event suit my donors?

- Do we have the skills to put on this type of event?
- Can we put on the event and raise money as well? What is the break-even point to raise money from the event?
- Do I need to raise all the money from ticket sales or will I have other fundraising on the night (for example, a raffle or charity auction)?

There are five key components to an event:

1. The people who will attend (the target audience).
2. The sponsors who may provide a free venue, discounted wine or auction prizes in exchange for exposure or access to your target audience.
3. The non-profit organisation and their internal resources who will benefit from the event.
4. The 'talent', i.e. the drawcard to the event. Perhaps a celebrity Master of Ceremonies (MC) or a popular entertainer.

Just like your overall fundraising strategy, you will want goals for your event. In particular, how much do you want to raise and from whom?

What to consider

Example: Say you want to run a $250 ticketed black-tie fundraising dinner to raise a net of $50,000.

To raise $50,000 you will need to sell a minimum of 200 tickets. This assumes you have no costs. If your costs are $10,000, you will need to sell 240 tickets to cover your costs and net $50,000. In order to sell 240 tickets, you will need to sell 24 tables each with 10 guests.

If you think you can raise money on the night in addition to ticket sales with raffles or an auction you could either reduce the individual ticket price or reduce the number of tickets you need to sell.

Before you commit to an event, consider whether you can get a good return on your investment. Remember our Value/Effort matrix? Events are often HIGH EFFORT FOR LOW VALUE. Try to reduce the effort and increase the value.

Event planning

To implement the event you need a plan and people to implement it. You need lots of arms and legs to implement it and cashflow to finance it.

You could organise an events team or person on staff to manage the event. You could make use of a volunteer committee (potentially a subcommittee of your foundation or organisation board) who can help sell tickets or tables, attract auction prizes and help run the event.

To be successful you'll need a few basics:

Consideration	Actions
The venue	Once you have the venue, you can commit to a date. The most attractive venues are often booked up well in advance. If you want the venue for free or at a reduced rate, talk to the owners early and see if you can get it on a date when it is less popular like mid-week rather than the weekend. This applies whether you are hosting a dinner or creating a cycling event. Don't assume the space you want will be available when you want it.
The date	Commit to a date. Nothing kills an event quicker than a date that keeps changing or is never decided upon. As soon as you've decided on the venue, commit to the date so you don't lose your location.

Consideration	Actions
The sponsors	Can you get someone to provide any of the necessary items for the event either free of charge or at a reduced rate? These are your sponsors. Consider who will print your tickets or programs or if you can get wine from a local supplier. As an example, printers or graphic designers will often help you out if it's a good cause and there may be more work for them in the future. Find suppliers who may be able to give you a good deal in exchange for promotion to your event attendees—perhaps feature them in the program or in other event collateral.
The audience	Choose your event to suit your audience. If you have a small number of high net worth donors, a Chairman's lunch or small dinner inviting a selected group of well-connected individuals may be more effective than trying to fill a ballroom with 300 people. If you have a large database of young individual donors, you could consider a more activity-based event like a fun run or a cultural or musical event.
The talent	What is going to attract sufficient numbers of people to attend your event apart from *it's for a good cause*? Can you get a well-liked comedian to be your MC? Does one of your board members know a famous actor who would attend if asked? Can you create an attractive and fun theme? Think about who will create interest with your audience and sell tickets.
The time	Do you have enough time to sell tickets and implement your event? Even small events (like a movie or trivia night) require a few months' lead time to plan and implement.
The return on investment	Can you make enough money from your event? Fundraising events should make a profit. How much profit do you need to generate to make the effort of the event worthwhile? Go back to the Value/Effort matrix and model, and consider whether the way you have designed your event will give you the most value for effort.

Consideration	Actions
The resources	Events take time, effort and money to implement. As you get better at them, this will reduce. However, the first time you put on an event it will likely be hard work. Do you have the resources to create a successful event? Can you pay for them?

14.6 Major gift and capital fundraising campaigns

We have talked about fundraising from individuals and you've learned that the greater the number of large gifts you receive, the fewer donors you need to reach your goal. You may wish to create a separate (but integrated) major gifts fundraising plan to focus on those donors who can give individual donations or grants in excess of $5,000 (a major donation).

When you have a large goal, for example, to raise the funds to build a new wing on a hospital or a new sports centre for a school, you could consider a capital fundraising campaign. Capital campaigns, which can aim to raise multi-millions of dollars, are implemented over many years and rely on building relationships with individuals as well as trustees of foundations and leveraging high profile and / or very committed volunteer leadership to promote and donate to the campaign.

This type of fundraising takes time, resources and money to successfully implement and often requires external assistance in the form of fundraising consultants or additional temporary resources in-house for the life of the campaign.

Feasibility studies

A feasibility study is a precursor to a capital campaign. It involves interviewing a selection of existing and potential donors to determine the feasibility of your campaign goals. Usually you share your draft Case for Support with interviewees and 'test' their response to it.

Why conduct a feasibility study?

Its aim is to help your organisation determine if you can identify sufficient potential lead volunteers and individual donors to support a significant fundraising goal. It informs you as to whether your campaign goal is feasible. This is an important step. It is a means of testing your Case for Support and your likelihood of raising all the funds. Before you spend thousands of dollars and many years trying to raise funds for a big capital development, test your idea with a small sample of your potential donors and ask them what they think about the project.

A feasibility study can help measure and determine:

- the internal 'campaign readiness' of your organisation: Do you have the right staff, volunteers, policies and procedures to implement the campaign?
- the level of support you can expect: Do you have sufficient donors or prospects with the means, interest and connection to the organisation? Can you identify volunteers who will donate to and lead the campaign?
- the campaign goal: Is your goal reasonable or too ambitious?
- the length of the campaign: How long will it take to raise the funds? How long do you actually have? How urgently must you raise the funds?

To implement a feasibility study you will need:

- a draft Case for Support to 'test' with prospective donors
- a list of prospective donors to interview

- a series of questions to ask donors about the project and your objectives
- an audit of the internal strengths and weaknesses of the organisation and, in particular, the fundraising or development office, to conduct the campaign.

Who implements a feasibility study?

Research recommends that capital campaigns should be tested with a feasibility study usually conducted by outside counsel, i.e. a fundraising consultancy that can engage with your donors and prospective donors in a non-biased way. A credible feasibility study is rarely conducted by the organisation's staff as it is hard for staff to remain objective (and quiet) during the interviews.[18]

Why use a fundraising consultancy?

For a feasibility study to have credibility, third-party professionals should construct it. There are many benefits to using a consultancy:

- Consultants can provide objectivity from outside evaluation and suggest solutions. You can share findings … the good, bad and the ugly.
- Individual prospects may not speak as candidly with organisation representatives and you will never know the vital information they wanted to share.
- Consultants supply the body of knowledge and industry best practice.
- Consultants have the necessary expertise and years of varied feasibility study experience to provide the guidance and discussion with prospective donors.

- Consultants can anticipate and potentially highlight or prevent problems for the charity.

- Consultants can facilitate discussion and decision-making. If this is done internally, discussions could be perceived as being biased coming from the department where the person sits.

- Experienced consultants have seen many examples of good and bad Cases for Support and you can benefit from their experience.

- Consultants can negotiate alignment across the board and staff.[19]

So what happens if your manager wants you to implement the feasibility study or sit in on the interviews? Here's some feedback you can give them:

- When staff sit in on feasibility interviews, some people cannot resist prompting, contradicting or even arguing with a prospect. As soon as the interviewee gets push-back, they stop giving their honest thoughts and the interview becomes pointless. A staff person doing the interview on their own would probably be oblivious to these effects and would make campaign assessments on inferior information.

- The more experienced the interviewer is in conducting feasibility studies, the better the result will be.

- A consultant's role is to be neutral, whereas a staffer has to represent the Board's views and organisation's vision.

Before you hire a fundraising consultancy to conduct your feasibility study (or help with any of your fundraising), you may want to ask certain questions:

- Have you done this before and with whom?

- What is your feasibility study methodology?
- Who will conduct the interviews (i.e. which specific consultant)?
- How many interviews should we undertake?
- Will you do the face-to-face interviews?
- Will you get a written summary of the interviews?
- Can you help us create a Case for Support to test?
- Can you show us examples of previous Cases for Support you have created?
- Will you be able to tell us whether we can reach our target?
- Can you speak to your past clients / referees?

Step 15: Doing it all

The bigger the strategy and the more ambitious the goals, the more likely you will need outside help. This could mean getting help with copywriting, design, strategic fundraising advice, telemarketing, direct mailing or printing. This is particularly true if you are using multiple channels to reach a broader cross-section of the community.

In most cases, you will need to do a bit of both. For example, if you want to produce high-quality marketing collateral materials, you may want to use a graphic designer, a copywriter and a printer.

15.1 Using outside suppliers

With fundraising and direct marketing activities, I recommend selecting suppliers who have experience working with similar clients or projects. Not all writers understand the requirements of direct response marketing or fundraising, and you don't want to waste your time and money finding that out or teaching them how to do it.

There are a great many websites where you can find freelancers who will bid for your work. Or you can find skilled volunteers to help you (but not if you're in a hurry as volunteers will work at their own pace and as time allows). Referrals will help you find suppliers who have the right experience and can deliver a good job.

15.2 A campaign brief

A campaign brief is a written document that articulates the work you want done. Each piece of work is often termed as a 'job'. You might send a brief to a printer, a copywriter or a graphic designer for a job you want done like printing a brochure, writing a direct mail letter or designing a logo. It is important to get in the habit of writing down what you want.

Getting quotes

Always ask for a written quote. Ask every supplier who you intend to pay to give you a written quote. That way you know exactly what you are getting for your money and how much it will cost. If they won't give you a written quote, if they are slow in providing a quote or if the quote contains minimal information, consider whether you want to use them. These are signs of what they may be like to work with, and these types of responses do not indicate a good way to start a working relationship.

It is equally important to consider how much you are willing to pay before you get the quote. That is where you can refer to your budget planning. I believe in telling suppliers how much you have to spend. It is highly unlikely that your budget will be too big for the job. It is usually the case that you have less money than is really needed. If you can tell the supplier how much you have to spend, you are likely to get a more tailored quote or they may tell you that you can't afford them. It's best to know this early. If you don't know how much you should pay for a particular job, ask around before you apply for quotes. There will be colleagues, peers and industry contacts to offer you general advice.

Once you have all the quotes (you may get multiple quotes if the jobs are large or expensive), you can decide the suppliers with whom you want to work. Having multiple quotes also lets you compare prices. Price should not be the only consideration but it is good to aim for value for money.

There are three ways a project (or job) can be implemented:

1. Fast (the quickest possible turnaround).
2. Cheap (the cheapest price).
3. Well (the highest quality).

You can sometimes get two out of three but rarely all three. Consider these when you are selecting your suppliers or volunteers.

- If you want something fast and cheap, it may not be done well.
- If you want it done well and cheap, it may not be fast.
- If you want it done well and fast, it may not be cheap.

What is your most important deliverable?

15.3 The implementation calendar

In order to implement your strategy, you need to allocate tasks with deadlines—even if you are intending to do everything yourself, your implementation calendar will help you with this. It is where you will plot actions that need to be taken, when and by whom.

The following example is an annual calendar but your fundraising strategy may only require a few weeks or months. One thing I've learned is that everything takes at least 30% longer than you anticipated, and that's assuming there isn't a crisis or other unexpected impact. For example, it takes at least eight weeks to create a direct mail campaign. You can do it faster but I always allow eight weeks to allow for delays in getting content, cleaning up lists or just getting the CEO to read and approve the letter copy.

For a magazine advertising campaign, it can take a month to generate the creative content, but there are long lead times for magazines so if you book the advertisement in January, you may not see your advertisement appear in the magazine until March or April. So again, you need to factor this into your planning. Even digital assets to put on a website or in an email campaign can take weeks to create depending on the skilled resources you have available. Make sure you allow time for this and allocate the person or organisation who will do the work.

Note: When working with external suppliers (printers, designers, writers, etc.), ensure your planning considers that these suppliers have other clients and you may not be their highest priority (I know, unimaginable, right?). If it will take five days for the actual work to be done, make sure you allow time to give the supplier a brief (a written document telling them what you want them to do), time for them to provide you with a quote, time for you to get comparison quotes then get the final quote approved, and time for the supplier to fit you into *their* calendar— assuming they can still do the job.

A five-day job can easily become a ten- or twenty-day turnaround if the supplier has other clients ahead of you, or if your organisation's internal processes are slow. This is not meant to dishearten you; it's designed to give you a sense of reality. Give yourself the time you need to do the best job possible. An example of a typical fundraising calendar is below.

ACTION / MONTH	Jan	Feb	Mar	Apr	May	Jun	Jul	Aug	Sept	Oct	Nov	Dec
Rent mailing list	X											
Write letter copy	X											
Agree photographs	X											
Print mail pack			X									
Test mail pack					X							
Lodge final mail pack						X						

15.4 Test. Test. Test.

Trust your results but keep testing. You always want to improve on your last results.

Possibly the main advantage to using direct response fundraising is that you can test efficacy with a small number of people without using your entire budget. Compared with, for example, a television campaign that requires a high up-front investment to produce a commercial before you even get it on air, a direct response campaign can be tested with a sample of your audience before you roll it out to your entire prospective donor list. A note here: don't let anyone persuade you to roll out a fundraising or telemarketing campaign to a huge mailing list without prior testing. Testing is a great way to discover if you have the right audience or segment and if you've asked for the right amount of money.

Many people will look at their response and only consider the amount of money raised. Of course, most of the time you want to raise more money than you spent on the campaign or you end up with a negative ROI. However, you can learn much more than that from every mailing you send out.

Here's an example of a test:

If you are intending to send a fundraising letter to 20,000 recipients, you can do a test with 1,000 recipients. If you receive 500 'return to senders', you have learned that there is something wrong with your mailing list. You may have a great offer but half of your recipients didn't receive it. While this is disappointing, you've learned that you need to fix your mailing list by getting the correct information or if you rented your list, talk to your supplier.

If, from the remaining 500 who did receive the mailing, you received a higher than average donation size or a larger response rate from a particular segment than you anticipated, you've learned two things: the mail pack worked *and* you need to fix your list. If you fix your list and resend the mail, you can anticipate a better response. If you had a less positive result than expected from those who responded, you have two problems: your list *and* your offer. Either way, it's much better to find this out before mailing everyone on your list of 20,000.

This is the clear benefit of direct response marketing. You can test. You will learn things you didn't expect. You can benefit from those learnings and keep testing. So before you roll out and spend your entire campaign budget in one hit, test as many elements of your fundraising campaign as you can. For example:

Type of Test	Features
Testing your email list	Test for email 'opens' (how many people opened it), 'bounce backs' (how many addresses were wrong), responses, number of donations and size of donations.
Testing your telemarketing list	Test for correct telephone numbers, positive and negative responses, and number and size of donations. Test what time or day you called, for example, whether it made a difference to call early morning or late afternoon, during the week or on the weekend.
Testing your coupon / response mechanism	Were all the details completed? Did you miss anything? Could you change / add anything? Can you accurately tell who returned the coupon or responded? Can you track visitors who received the mailing to your website?
Creative execution or offer	A/B testing: Test different creative executions or offers and compare the results when they are sent to different segments. Do this before you roll out your full campaign. It can be used with most direct response channels.

With the results you gain from your tests, update your strategy and make any relevant changes to your implementation.

Measurability

You can measure whether you've been successful by the response mechanism you use. This is the most fascinating (and sometimes infuriating) benefit of direct response marketing. If you send out a mail pack to 1,000 people (and you've created a functioning response mechanism), you will get a response that ranges from '0' (no one replied) to some percentage response rate from your 1,000 recipients.

Whatever your definition of success (and of course you have defined your goals, haven't you?), you will know whether you have reached it because direct response provides measurable results.

You can measure results in a number of ways:

- Number of direct mail coupons returned.
- Number of phone calls received.
- Number of emails received.
- Average size of donation.
- Number of donations.
- Largest donation.
- Smallest donation.
- Number of 'return to senders'.

Step 16: Caring for donor data

Whether you collect details about people you would like to donate to you or people who already donate, you need a place to keep that information. Everyone you engage with has a reasonable expectation that your organisation will operate ethically and with honesty. This includes how you collect, manage and use their data. You can call it a CRM system, a database or a donor management system—whatever the name, it's a place where you can store and retrieve data (information) about your donors.

Your fundraising hinges on your capacity to capture and manipulate data. Why? Because if you can't measure how your fundraising is working and who does or will donate to you, how will you know how much to invest or who to invest in? You also won't be able to report to your management about how funds have been spent or how much you've raised, which makes it more difficult to ask for more funds to invest. Essentially, you need a manageable list of people with whom to fundraise.

Managing data

Most organisations start managing data with that evil genius, the Excel spreadsheet. While it is a good place to begin, it is not a tool on which to become reliant. You can store and sort data in Excel, but unless you are an expert it can be difficult to maintain and retrieve data. So, as soon as you can, move to a dedicated system that allows you to get a better view of your data.

There are multiple CRM or database options available (free or expensive). The type of system you choose will depend on:

- The amount of data you want to capture.
- The types of activities you want to track.
- The amount of money you have to invest in a system.
- Whether you need to manage it yourself or have a data management specialist (or a willing volunteer) to look after it.

Regardless of the system you choose, ensure you can easily sort and retrieve the data you enter. There is limited value in collecting data if you can't sort it and make use of it. Data also has an annoying habit of getting old quickly so you need to maintain it and keep it up to date. You'd be surprised how many phone numbers or email addresses can change in three months; therefore, use it or lose it.

Make the data work for you. Use it to:

- Create categories, for example, donor types (regular, one-off, high net worth).
- Customise the information you send out.
- Solicit different levels of gifts.
- Separate donors from prospective donors.

- Separate individual donors from trusts and foundations or corporations.

16.1 Donor financial data

When you attract a donation to your cause, you will need to capture information about the donor. The financial transaction may be captured by your bookkeeper or accountant or finance team. The fundraising team will also need to capture the contact information about your donor as well as any notes you want to keep about that donor.

If at all possible, track financial donation data in the same system you keep your donor information. Many hours can be spent trying to match financial records in finance systems against donor spreadsheets. Work with your finance team, accountant or bookkeeper to set up a system where you can have the most transparency around your donations and minimise double handling.

16.2 Prospect data

If you don't have donors yet, you will want to start keeping information on your prospects. Then, as you ask them for donations and they start to donate, you can update their records and keep a track of their transactions and relationship with you.

At a minimum, you will want to keep the following record on each donor or prospect:

- First name and family name.
- Date of birth / age.
- Date when first acquired.
- How you acquired the name.
- Home address.

- Postal address.

- Contact number.

- Email address.

- Date of last gift.

- Size of last gift.

- Project / appeal they responded to.

- A record of conversations with them.

16.3 Donor privacy and data protection

There are laws, regulations and best practice with how you manage data.

Here is an overview of things you should consider:

Permission: Before you send someone your newsletter or a direct mail letter, you need their permission to add them to your mailing list. If you've rented their data, ensure that the company from which you've hired the list has the permission of those on the list.

Privacy law: All charities are governed by the privacy laws of the countries in which they operate. Visit your local government website for more information.

Policies and procedures: Your organisation should have policies and procedures that help your leadership understand how to care for your donors' data even if you're not required to comply with the Privacy Act. For guidance, you can visit government websites or you can view policies of similar or like-minded organisations. Organisations that communicate effectively will have their policies (particularly those relating to data management) publicly available on their website.

Opt-out vs opt-in: You can choose when to give your community an 'opt-in' or an 'opt-out'. When you ask someone to 'opt-in', they need to give their permission before you add them to a list or send them communications. If they 'opt-out' they get added to a list and / or receive information but have the choice to 'opt-out' so as not to receive future material.

SUMMARY

How will you know when you are ready to implement your plan?

Your SMART goals will indicate the target dates for when you need to deliver your result but what about knowing when to start. Do not wait until you have all your 'ducks in a row' because that day will never come. So how *do* you know when to start?

You have written your plan

As of today, you have written a plan that is as good as you can get it. Maybe it'll be better tomorrow, but today you have a well-thought-out plan and you know what actions you need to take.

You have the budget

When you have the budget to implement the methodology, you can get started. Even if you don't have all of the money straight away, you know that it will come.

You have some of the key resources

Let's face it, you'll never have *all* the resources you'd like. So long as you have a good percentage of them (and whatever is missing will not create a 'hinge factor'[20]), you can get started with your fundraising strategy.

Stage 4

Evaluate your fundraising strategy

*'Unless strategy evaluation is performed
seriously and systematically, and
unless strategists are willing to
act on the results, energy will be
used up defending yesterday.'*

—Peter Drucker

EVALUATE YOUR FUNDRAISING STRATEGY

Congratulations! You have planned, written and implemented your fundraising strategy. In order to evaluate how well you did and how close you came to achieving or even exceeding your goals, you will put measures in place and plan for any unexpected contingencies.

If you have prepared carefully and implemented your campaign well, you should start seeing some results as soon as you implement your strategy. You may get a sudden flurry of activity or a gentle trickle.

In Stage 4, we work through the final steps to build evaluation into your strategy. You can learn something from all your results and, with clear objectives, you can compare these with your response. Be prepared to capture these results in your CRM system or at least in an Excel spreadsheet.

4-STAGE FUNDRAISING STRATEGY		
STEP	**DESCRIPTION**	**YOUR PROGRESS**
	Stage 4: Evaluate your fundraising strategy	
17	Measures of success 17.1 KPI dashboard 17.2 Return on investment (ROI) 17.3 Donor lifetime value	
18	Donor stewardship	
19	Ethics and accountability 19.1 Donor Charter and Donor Bill of Rights	
20	Contingency planning and risk management	

Step 17: Measures of success

You set goals at the outset of your strategy in order to motivate yourself to deliver them and measure results against them. As you implement your strategy, it is helpful to create a dashboard of the measures you will use to evaluate success. If you have set clear goals, you should be able to accurately measure whether you have achieved them.

The most important measure of success once you have implemented your strategy is to compare your results with your SMART goals. How close did you come to achieving them? You may like to include sub-goals or another measure of success that helps you measure results that aren't solely about income. You could consider referencing some of the fundraising principles at the beginning of this book.

17.1 KPI dashboard

Set up a KPI (Key Performance Indicator) dashboard to clearly show how well your fundraising strategy went. This links to your goals, and after you have implemented your strategy, you can add how you went here. You can add if you did not implement some of your planned activities. This is a good place to make general notes, for example, the direct mail pack planned for lapsed donors was not sent out.

Quantitative KPI dashboard

On a scale of 1 to 5, where 1 is 'Poor' and 5 is 'Excellent', answer these questions:

Measure / goal	Original goal	Not achieved (0)	Achieved (1–4)	Exceeded (5)	Notes
Financial income goals					
Non-financial goals					
• Total value of gifts					
• Total number of gifts					
• Total average value of gifts					
• Total number of new donors					
• Total number of returned donors					
Total expenditure budget					
ROI by channel or donor segment					
Expenditure by individual channel					
Over all return on investment					

Qualitative KPIs

You can also try to measure qualitative goals such as the following:

Measure / goal	Not achieved (0)	Achieved (1–4)	Exceeded (5)	Notes
How well did our team work with other stakeholders?				
How does our fundraising strategy integrate with the organisational strategy?				
Can our leadership team see how much will be raised and spent on the strategy?				
How well did we ask for money?				

17.2. Return on investment (ROI)

ROI is a financial ratio used to calculate the benefit earned from the investment you make in your fundraising. The higher the ratio, the greater the benefit earned. When an investment shows a positive or negative ROI, it can indicate the value of your investment. Of course you will want to make friends, build relationships and engage with your donors. However, if you don't generate more than you invest, you will always feel like you are chasing your tail, needing to raise more money all the time. Eventually your organisation will become financially unsustainable.

ROI is your net income divided by the financial investment (costs). Gross income is the money you raise before deducting costs. Net income is the funds you raise after deducting costs; therefore, *gross income – costs = net income* and *net income* / costs = *ROI*.

Here is an example: If you generate a gross of $150,000 and deduct costs of $50,000 you will have a net income of $100,000. Your ROI is $100,000 / $50,000 x 100% = 200%. So you achieve a positive 200% ROI.

While ROI is a useful measure, it does not consider that other important investment: **time**. Consider how long it will take to deliver the hoped-for ROI: A month, a year, a decade? The time it will take to deliver the result is useful additional information to the ROI measurement. You may prefer to accept a lower ROI in a shorter period than wait for a better return over a longer period or vice versa.

In addition, it is important to be consistent with the expenses included in the costs. If you are comparing the potential ROI of two marketing channels, ensure you compare apples with apples by measuring the same costs for each channel. It is sometimes tempting to leave out certain costs in order to make the ROI look better, but in the long term it won't help you achieve your results.

17.3 Donor lifetime value

Lifetime value (LTV) is the cumulative value of your donors' contributions over the life of their support of your cause. One formula used for measuring donor lifetime value is to take their average donation total multiplied by the average number of donations in a year multiplied by average donor retention time in years. This provides the average lifetime value of a donor based on your existing data.

As an example, if 60% of your donors on average donate $100 a year and the average retention rate is five years, the individual donor lifetime value is $500. Imagine if this were $1,000 or even $10,000. Using the same scenario, one of your goals could be to measure your current average LTV then increase it to six or ten years by improving your donor engagement practices. You can hopefully begin to see how looking at the cumulative value of your donors is an important measure once you have a few years' donor data to analyse.

You can also apply this analysis to different donor segments and you will find that some donor segments return a better lifetime value than others. This can help you understand how to invest your fundraising budget in future strategies and campaigns.

LTV can also help identify donors who, by looking at individual gifts, may appear to be 'small' donors but when you consider their lifetime value, a different picture emerges. Note: Any donor who gives every year for multiple years is worth significant attention no matter the size of the individual gift. This cannot be overstated. Half your donors will only ever give once so our job is both to encourage repeat gifts and look after loyal donors through effective stewardship.

Step 18: Donor stewardship

Having gone to so much effort to attract donors, the absolute best use of your time and money now is to keep as many of them as possible and encourage them to donate again by looking after them. This is called donor stewardship and it is the final stage in our donor giving cycle before we recommence the cultivation process. Holding on to donors (retention) should be your mantra. Any research you read about selling will confirm that it costs ten times more to acquire a new customer than to keep an existing one. So looking after donors is vital to the health of your organisation and to maintain a respectful relationship with your communities.

Keeping your donors happy, willing to give and encouraged by the work you do should be your primary focus. If you have happy donors, you have a successful organisation and successful fundraising campaigns. You cannot overdo this. You cannot thank your donors too much. You cannot smile or laugh too much. 'Over the top' is better than 'underdone'. Love them every day. You'll enjoy your job more, and you'll do better work for your organisation.

Effective stewardship and accountability

When we think of a 'steward' we imagine a friendly, polite and helpful person in white gloves. That is a good image as we should be treating our donors in a polite, friendly way, effectively acquitting their donations and ensuring they feel well looked after. Effective stewardship means we track and record donor contributions to ensure they are used as the donor intends. It also means that we respond to and thank donors in a timely way, recognising and reporting results and impact, ensuring donor privacy and protecting donor rights. It may sound like a lot but it is essential if we expect loyalty from our donors.

Stewardship and accountability are key issues that build trust for all non-profit organisations; however, it is often an area that is given insufficient attention as dollars and income take precedence. Is it any wonder that so few donors make a second donation?

Donors as friends

Do you have acquaintances who, when you see their number appear on your phone, you sigh and think *what do they want?* This is how a lot of donors respond when your organisation's number appears on their phone or your email appears in their inbox. Do you want to be one of 'those' friends? Wouldn't you rather people want to take your call because you might have something interesting to say or because they like talking with you?

The things you do to retain and engage your friends are also the things you can do to keep your donors. Consider the following and ask yourself when the last time was an organisation you support (or used to support) did any of them:

- Called you by your preferred name (they didn't just assume James is Jim and Margaret is Maggie).
- Called to say hi and to thank you for your support (without asking for another donation).
- Recognised your birthday.
- Acknowledged your gift with a personal note.
- Called and invited you for a coffee (even if it were to see the organisation's latest project).
- Called to see how you are and how your life is going.
- Recognised the anniversary of your first gift.
- Called to update you on a project you have helped fund.
- Wrote a personal note to you regarding the next campaign update.
- Acknowledged a major milestone in your life like an award, a marriage or a promotion.

If you think that some of these are over the top, stop and think about it. Why should someone continue giving their support or consider you to be part of their lives if you only ever communicate with them when you want their money? Would you keep a friend like this?

Our relationships with our donors need a reboot. Okay, not everyone wants a phone call from all of the charities they support. But perhaps they would like to hear from the ones that are most important to them. I have supported several organisations for decades and I have never (without exception) received a call from the CEO or fundraising director thanking me for my gift or acknowledging my long-term support. Don't you think that after 20 years of giving, I might be a major donor prospect or a bequest prospect? Not if you don't engage with me. (NB: phone calls welcome ☺.)

Why do we take this approach with our donors? Donors are very hard to find and it's often expensive to convert them from prospects to financial supporters. So once we get them, why do we ignore them? Those who have chosen to support our organisation over others should be cherished. They have indicated that our organisation is important to them and that our cause means something to them. They give because something resonates within them.

So pick up on that vibration and follow up with them. Make the effort to understand why they have supported you. Continue to give them feedback so they continue to benefit from that resonation. No one donates without some interest in the cause they are supporting. Full stop. Donors are active participants in your cause. They are not passive benefactors no matter how low their level of engagement. They are your lifeblood. Never ever forget this.

Step 19: Ethics and accountability

An organisation's ability to operate correlates with the confidence and trust the public has in it. All organisations have a duty to maintain public confidence. The public wants to be assured that your organisation runs quality programs in an ethical manner.

All donors have a reasonable expectation to understand how a gift will be used and what outcomes may be expected from the organisation; therefore, every effort should be made to honour the donor's intent regardless if the gift is restricted or unrestricted.

The continuance of our organisations relies on our donors' trust in us and we need to provide evidence to our donors that their trust is not misplaced.

19.1 Donor Charter and Donor Bill of Rights

Some organisations have committed to a Donor Charter or Donor Bill of Rights and they promote these in publications and on their websites. The Donor Bill of Rights sets forth that donors have the right, 'To be informed of the organization's mission, of the way the organization intends to use donated resources, and of its capacity to use donations effectively for their intended purposes'.

The Donor Bill of Rights was created by the Association of Fundraising Professionals (AFP) the Association for Healthcare Philanthropy (AHP), the Council for Advancement and Support of Education (CASE) and The Giving Institute.[21] It gives donors the right to be informed of the mission and who is serving on the board and to expect good judgement in the board's stewardship responsibilities. It also gives the right to have access to the organisation's most recent financial statements.

These represent public commitments to an organisation's donors to provide outstanding levels of donor stewardship to ensure donors have a positive, ethical experience when dealing with the organisation.

Step 20: Contingency planning and risk management

Even with the best plan (and your plan will be great), it is important to consider contingencies to deal with any risk.

To help you assess the degree of risk and how you will deal with it, you can complete a risk analysis register. Your organisation may already have a register relating to its overall operations. However, you can create one for your fundraising strategy to help you think ahead and plan for the worst while hoping for the best.

Your risk register would ask these questions:

The type of risk	The impact of the risk occurring	The likelihood of the risk occurring (1 = low likelihood / 5 = high likelihood)	How the risk will be mitigated
Risks can take the form of internal or external risks. The chance of your boss deciding to cut your budget is an internal risk; the chance of a pandemic is an external risk. A few years ago we would have thought the risk of a pandemic to be very low. Well, it just shows you how situations can change. You do not have to capture every potential catastrophe but consider those that would have a major impact on your strategy if they were to occur and, importantly, how you could mitigate the risk of it happening, if at all.	Some impacts will be greater than others. Consider what would happen if your expenditure budget was reduced or a major event needed to be cancelled at the last minute. What would happen to your results if this risk occurred?	Few of us could have imagined the pandemic or the previous global financial crisis (GFC). We need to think harder about events that may happen within or outside our organisations and rank the likelihood of them happening. If you live far enough inland, the risk of flood will be low. However, if you live in a bushfire prone area, the risk of a major bushfire disrupting your work (and possibly your life) plans could be high. While you are capturing each risk, note down why you ranked it as likely or not.	Now comes the fun part that takes some creative thinking. You need to imagine the risk actually happening and consider what can be done BEFORE it happens to minimise the negative impact. We can all be wiser after the event—hindsight is a wonderful thing. It takes practice to consider what may happen and put in place actions that would minimise the impact.

Here are some examples:

The type of risk	The impact of the risk occurring	The likelihood of the risk occurring (1 = low / 5 = high)	Why this likelihood ranking?	How the risk will be mitigated
My budget is reduced by 30%.	I could implement only part of my fundraising strategy.	2	We have just confirmed all of our budgets for the year.	I will take my manager through my strategy so she understands the importance of the entire program. I will break down my budget sufficiently to understand where I get my best ROI to focus on these areas if I have fewer funds to invest.
My fundraising dinner is cancelled due to COVID-19 restrictions.	I would raise less money and would need to pay some costs I cannot recoup.	4	There are still intermittent lockdowns and restrictions being announced.	I will create a virtual event back-up plan to host the event online if needed. I will notify my donors of the possibility and get them on board. I will work with suppliers in advance to negotiate refunds or better payment terms.

The type of risk	The impact of the risk occurring	The likelihood of the risk occurring (1 = low / 5 = high)	Why this likelihood ranking?	How the risk will be mitigated
My website goes down due to hacking.	I would raise less money. I would lose one of my key communication channels. My online channels would be at risk.	3	We have anti-hacking software in place and a very effective IT department that monitors activity.	I will ensure my donor CRM system is up to date with emails and postal addresses so I can contact my community. I will diversify my fundraising strategy so I am not overly reliant on digital channels for income.

CONCLUSION

Congratulations! You have now completed your strategy. You know who you want to raise funds from and why people should donate. You understand your cause and the resources you have to apply to your strategy. By this stage, you have learned about the donors you want to attract, the channels you will use and how effective your strategy will be in achieving your goals. What a great result!

But don't stop now. Make sure you share your strategy with your colleagues and get their input. Use it to help others in your organisation understand the benefits of a strategic fundraising plan to raise more money and help your organisation deliver on its mission.

BRINGING IT ALL TOGETHER

I wrote this book because I wanted to share what I have learned during my working life, of which more than 20 years has been spent with the not-for-profit sector. Many things have changed in that time. We have seen the revolution of the internet and the increased need for additional support in almost every area of our work from medical research to emergency relief whether from the most recent pandemic or from the changes wrought from climate change. We have seen the development of structured giving with philanthropists making their donations.

In reading this book, you have learned that there are systems and strategies you can put in place that will help you to achieve great things with your fundraising. Fundraising does not need to be a 'dark art' or remain mysterious. By taking a systematic approach to your fundraising strategy, you will learn so much about how to improve your results and deliver so much more for your organisation.

By reading this book, you are investing in your own professional development. You are taking responsibility for the outcomes you produce and providing yourself with the tools to get the job done. One aim of this book is to help you to learn the techniques and subtleties of writing a fundraising strategy as the most effective way to deliver on your goals. Your organisational goals and your vision for your future are the most important assets you have to achieve your fundraising outcomes.

With a fundraising strategy you have a means of telling your story—your vision—to a wider group of people. The more people who know about you, the more you can inspire them to act and the more likely it is you will raise more money.

This book is set out in stages, and if you follow this approach, you will have a consistent, long-lasting strategy that you can update once a year or every couple of years.

In Stage 1 you prepared your strategy by bringing all the information you need together in one place. It is the research you need to inform your strategy.

In Stage 2 you wrote your strategy by pulling all the pieces together. Here you captured your goals and how you will go about reaching them.

In Stage 3 you implemented your strategy and learned many things along the way.

In Stage 4 you evaluated your results, assessed how you did things and decided whether you will make any changes in the future.

If you truly want to maximise what you spend and the results you can achieve, follow the guidance of this book and write a fundraising strategy.

A last thought: What do you want to be remembered for? If you have a vision for your organisation, this book provides you with the means—a clear strategy—to bring it to life. We should all strive for excellence and deliver the best we can. As the strategy guru Peter Drucker says, 'The chief factor for achieving success is accountability'. That means holding yourself accountable.[22]

With a clear, written strategy, you have a better chance of achieving this.

I wish you well, and I thank you for letting me be a part of your journey.

Please write to me at pamela@fundraiserhandbook.com and tell me how you are doing and what you've learned. Let me know what you achieve. I'd love to hear about your results.

Remember … keep focused and keep fundraising.

APPENDICES

APPENDIX 1: Terms and Definitions

APPENDIX 2: Preparing Your Fundraising Strategy

APPENDIX 3: Fundraising Strategy Template

APPENDIX 4: Budget Breakdown

APPENDIX 5: Segmented Channel Activation

APPENDIX 6: Implementation Calendar

APPENDIX 7: Example Bequest Wording

APPENDIX 8: Evaluation Dashboard

APPENDIX 1: TERMS AND DEFINITIONS

TERM	DEFINITION
Acquisition	The process for attracting donors.
Ambassador	High profile individuals who assist with fundraising campaigns. Ambassadors are recruited for a specific period and may have made a significant financial donation.
Bequest	A donation provided in a supporter's will and received by a beneficiary organisation after the donor's death.
Business Case	A document for internal stakeholders. The proposition for which you are raising funds, the detailed figures and analysis of why this is the best way forward, and how and why your organisation should invest in it.
Capital Campaign	A major gift campaign conducted over a period to attract significant donations for a major project, for example, a new school building.
Case for Support	A printed or digital document that outlines the case behind the need to raise funds. A Case for Support is utilised with major donors as part of the cultivation process.
Confirmed Bequest	A living supporter who has confirmed in writing that they have included a beneficiary organisation in their will.
Cultivation	Part of the Donor Development Cycle is to cultivate a relationship with a prospective donor prior to soliciting a donation.
Donor	Any supporter making a tax-deductible donation of any value. Donations of $2.00 or more are tax deductible in Australia.
Donor Giving Cycle	The process of bringing a prospective donor through a series of steps resulting in a gift then stewarding that donor to their next gift, forming a cycle. Sometimes referred to as *moves management*.

APPENDIX 1: TERMS AND DEFINITIONS

TERM	DEFINITION
Donor Loyalty	A measure of how connected donors are to the organisation. Measured by time and / or dollars donated.
Feasibility Study	A face-to-face research study with potential donors to help ascertain the potential for success in securing leadership gifts for the campaign. Helps decide on timing and target of a proposed capital campaign.
Fundraising Appeals and Campaigns	Communicating with donors, prospects and members requesting a donation via direct mail, telemarketing, onsite and online as part of a planned strategic campaign.
Gift	Another word for donation.
Gift Chart	Ways of clarifying what gifts are needed at what level. Also can be used to a) track progress and b) share in part with donors if they'd like to consider at what level they would like to donate.
L.I.C.	An acronym for a prospect qualification process: Link, Inclined and Capacity to Give (L.I.C.) of your prospective donors.
Lifetime Value (LTV)	The cumulative financial value of all donations over the 'life' of a donor's support for the organisation.
Member	Visitors buy annual membership that allows entry to an organisation, for example, art gallery or zoological gardens. Memberships are usually not considered tax-deductible donations as the member receives a benefit. Strictly speaking, members are not donors but they may consider themselves as such.
NFP	Not-for-profit / Non-profit
Public Phase	The public phase of a campaign aims to engage the community with a view to securing multiple donations. The public phase of a fundraising campaign is planned to commence when a minimum of 50% of the capital campaign goal has been reached and it fits with the organisation's strategic objectives.

TERM	DEFINITION
Quiet Phase	The early stage of a capital campaign before it goes 'public'. The quiet phase is the time when the very large donations are secured.
Regular Donors	Regular Donors are financial donors who have made a commitment to make a regular, periodic payment (monthly, quarterly or annually), usually by credit card as an automatic deduction. These donors have become the foundation of many successful donor cultivation strategies.
Retention	A strategy to retain as many donors as possible as active donors.
Return on Investment (ROI)	The calculation to determine the benefit for your fundraising investment.
Solicitation	Part of the Donor Development Cycle to ask a prospective donor for a gift or donation.
Sponsor	Corporations that are looking for status and benefits in return for giving a financial or in-kind contribution towards an NFP organisation.
Stewardship	Looking after donors after they have made a gift. Stewarding their relationship with the organisation potentially towards a further gift. Ensuring they have a positive relationship with the organisation they have supported.
Tied / Restricted Donations	The donation is allocated to a specific approved project that is part of the (organisation) strategic capital plan. Specific projects are promoted to donors.
Untied / Unrestricted Donations	The donation is a general donation to an organisation, the use of which is at the organisation's discretion.
Volunteer	A person who donates their time to a not-for-profit organisation without charge. Usually someone with a commitment to the cause who wants to assist. Sometimes utilised in the Donor Development Cycle.

APPENDIX 2: PREPARING YOUR FUNDRAISING STRATEGY

Priority	Question	What do we want to know?	Answer	Additional comments
1. Internal resources	What do you have to work with in terms of the following resources? • Money • Time • People • Tools	How much can we spend? How much do we want to raise? How much time do we have? Who / what can help us?	Detail here as much information as you have.	Are there any comments or feedback or internal knowledge that you should document that might impact your strategy?
2. What are you raising the money for?	What is your project?	What's your Case for Support?	Why should anyone give to you? How will you spend the money you raise? How long will it take to achieve your goals?	Are there any issues or conditions related to the project(s)? Who makes decisions on what you raise funds for?
3. Who is likely to fund your project?	Who's your target audience?	Who are your donors and prospects?	Specifically, how many of each category of donor / prospect do you have? Make lists of the different categories / segments and capture everything you know about them.	Consider whether you will get donations from the board, the senior team, any committees, volunteers, current donors, prospective donors, corporate sponsors, or trusts and foundations.

APPENDIX 3: FUNDRAISING STRATEGY TEMPLATE

4-STAGE FUNDRAISING STRATEGY		
STEP	**DESCRIPTION**	**YOUR PROGRESS**
Stage 1: Prepare your fundraising strategy		
1	Current situation 1.1 Vision and mission 1.2 Key stakeholders 1.3 Key deadlines	
2	Related policies and procedures	
3	Situation analysis 3.1 Where you are now 3.2 Why are you raising money? What needs will you meet? 3.3 What projects need funding? 3.4 What's your Case for Support? 3.5 Who are you and why should you be doing this work? 3.6 Who will implement the work on the ground? 3.7 How much will it cost to implement the work? 3.8 Why should anyone support your cause?	
4	Resources 4.1 People (paid staff and volunteers) 4.2 Tools 4.3 Time 4.4 Money	
5	Analysing donors and prospects 5.1 Existing donors and prospects 5.2 Developing demographic donor profiles 5.3 Profiling and qualifying prospects 5.4 Donor acquisition	

4-STAGE FUNDRAISING STRATEGY		
STEP	**DESCRIPTION**	**YOUR PROGRESS**
Stage 2: Write your fundraising strategy		
6	Strategic approach and competitive advantage	
7	Your unique selling proposition (USP)	
8	SMART goals and objectives	
9	Determine your target audience/s 9.1 Turning suspects into advocates: the Ladder of Loyalty 9.2 The donor pyramid 9.3 Donor retention and growth	
10	Fundraising income and expenditure budget 10.1 Budget by type of donor 10.2 Budget by marketing channel 10.3 Determine your net return	
Stage 3: Implement your fundraising strategy		
11	Attract donors' attention: the AIDA Principle	
12	Determine marketing and fundraising channels 12.1 Direct response marketing vs mass marketing 12.2 Direct marketing appeals or campaign structure 12.3 Digital fundraising 12.4 Channel integration	
13	The Value/Effort matrix	
14	Create targeted fundraising plans 14.1 Structured campaigns and fundraising appeals 14.2 Developing a bequests, gifts in wills or legacies plan 14.3 Grants (applications to trusts and foundations) 14.4 Corporate sponsorship 14.5 Events 14.6 Major gift and capital fundraising campaigns	

4-STAGE FUNDRAISING STRATEGY		
STEP	**DESCRIPTION**	**YOUR PROGRESS**
15	Doing it all 15.1 Using outside suppliers 15.2 A campaign brief 15.3 The implementation calendar 15.4 Test. Test. Test.	
16	Caring for donor data 16.1 Donor financial data 16.2 Prospect data 16.3 Donor privacy and data protection	
Stage 4: Evaluate your fundraising strategy		
17	Measures of success 17.1 KPI dashboard 17.2 Return on investment (ROI) 17.3 Donor lifetime value	
18	Donor stewardship	
19	Ethics and accountability 19.1 Donor Charter and Donor Bill of Rights	
20	Contingency planning and risk management	

APPENDIX 4: BUDGET BREAKDOWN

Type of donor	Targeted amount	Average donation	Number of donations required	Expenditure budget	Total to be raised	Net return	NET ROI for every $1.00 invested
Individual donors (giving <$500)							
Individual donors (giving >$500)							
Corporations							
Trusts and foundations							
Bequests							
Totals							

APPENDIX 5: SEGMENTED CHANNEL ACTIVATION

Target audience	Number of prospects targeted	Email	Telemarketing	Direct mail	TV / radio	Social media	Website	Face to face
Current donors (donated <$1,000 in the last 12 months)								
Prospective donors (never donated)								
Past donors (donated <$1,000 over 12 months ago)								
Trusts and foundations (never applied to before)								
Trusts and foundations (unsuccessfully applied)								
Trusts and foundations (successfully applied)								
Major donors (donated >$1,000 ever)								

Target audience	Number of prospects targeted	Email	Telemarketing	Direct mail	TV / radio	Social media	Website	Face to face
Major donors (never donated)								
Corporate sponsorship								

APPENDIX 6: IMPLEMENTATION CALENDAR

ACTION / MONTH	Jan	Feb	Mar	Apr	May	Jun	Jul	Aug	Sept	Oct	Nov	Dec

APPENDIX 7: EXAMPLE BEQUEST WORDING

'I give (proportion of estate or dollar amount or the residue of my estate) free of all taxes to the (ORGANISATION in STATE, TERRITORY OR COUNTRY) for its use and benefit absolutely.'

'I give (clearly describe the amount, asset, item, work of art, manuscript, etc.) free of all taxes to the (ORGANISATION in STATE, TERRITORY OR COUNTRY) for its use and benefit absolutely.'

'I give (proportion of estate or dollar amount or residue of my estate or clearly described item) to (names of primary beneficiaries) but if (all primary beneficiaries) predecease me, then to the (ORGANISATION in STATE, TERRITORY OR COUNTRY free of all taxes.'

APPENDIX 8: EVALUATION DASHBOARD

Measure / goal	Not achieved (0)	Achieved (1–4)	Exceeded (5)	Notes
Financial income goals				
Non-financial goals				
• Total value of gifts				
• Total number of gifts				
• Total average value of gifts				
• Total number of new donors				
• Total number of returned donors				
Total expenditure budget				
ROI by channel or donor segment				
Expenditure by individual channel				
Overall return on investment				

BIBLIOGRAPHY AND SOURCES

A Grant-Seeker's Guide to Trusts & Foundations

Author: **Vanessa Meachen**

The word 'philanthropy' is often used but many people find the world of philanthropy quite mysterious. There are many different meanings to the word, usually depending on who you ask. In the context of this guide, we will be using Philanthropy Australia's definition, which is: the planned and structured giving.

A Guide to Giving for Australians

Author: **Philanthropy Australia**

This is a comprehensive guide to philanthropy for donors, proudly supported by the Myer Foundation. It is a useful resource for anyone who would like to be involved in giving in Australia, from businesses thinking of setting up a charitable foundation to individuals who would like to leave money in their will.

An Introductory Guide to Grantmaking

Author: **Vanessa Meachen**

This practical guide outlines the role of grant-makers, working practices and cycles, assessing applications and communication tools. Information on further resources is also provided.

Directory of Funders

Author: **Philanthropy Australia**

185

An essential online resource for not-for-profit organisations, charities and community groups.

Genderwise Philanthropy Guide

Author: **Australian Women Donors Network**

Strengthening society by investing in women and girls, this guide is an easy-to-read approach to inclusive giving.

PRESSing Matters

Author: **Philanthropy Australia**

Up until July 2015, PRESSing Matters was PA's weekly media monitoring service for Members and Associates. This service is now incorporated in Philanthropy Weekly epublication, bringing you the latest news clippings, major donations, grant rounds, initiatives, appointments and opportunities, co-partnerships, policy & research updates, events and more.

Private Ancillary Funds (PAF) Trustee Handbook

Author: **David Ward, Treasurer, Philanthropy Australia**

Comments on what is required of the trustee, and directors thereof, of PAFs under the Guidelines and at law. It is not a legal document but a 'plain English' introductory guide to the role and duties of the trustee(s) and all directors.

Public Ancillary Funds (PuAF) Trustee Handbook

Author: **David Ward, Treasurer, Philanthropy Australia**

What is now required of trustees of PuAFs, and where the trustee is a company the directors thereof, under the Guidelines and at law. It is not a legal document but a 'plain English' introductory guide to the role and duties of the trustee and trustee directors.

Savvy Giving: The Art and Science of Philanthropy

Author: **Genevieve Timmons**

Commissioned by Australian Communities Foundation, this book offers inspiring guidance for anyone involved in a charitable giving program. By using both the head and the heart, this book offers a step-by-step guide on how you can achieve impact and an enduring benefit from every dollar.

Trustee Handbook: Roles & Duties of Trustees of Charitable Trusts & Foundations in Australia (2nd)

Author: **David Ward, Treasurer, Philanthropy Australia**

Created in consultation with Philanthropy Australia's Members, this Trustee Handbook is an essential document for Private Charitable Funds, Ancillary Funds, Family Foundations and Community Foundations. It covers types of foundations, legislation, governance, administration, investment, distribution / grantmaking, Responsible Person outline, trustee dossier guidelines and more.

ENDNOTES

1. Picco, G. (2020, June 19). *Canadian charity trends in direct mail*. The Charity Report. Retrieved 23 November 2021, from https://www.thecharityreport.com/news/canadian-charity-trends-in-direct-mail/

2. *Quarterly COVID charity tracker survey results*. (2021, June 17). Pro Bono Economics. Retrieved 23 November 2021, from https://www.probonoeconomics.com/quarterly-covid-charity-tracker-survey-results-april-2021

3. Bekkers, R., & Wiepking, P. (2010). A literature review of empirical studies of philanthropy. *Nonprofit and Voluntary Sector Quarterly*, 40(5), 924–973. https://doi.org/10.1177/0899764010380927

4. Charities Aid Foundation. (n.d.). *Charitable giving in Australia 2019: How people give*. Retrieved 23 November 2021, from https://www.cafonline.org/about-us/publications/2019-publications/australia-giving-2019

5. Vincent, C. (2019, July 30). *Pareto fundraising benchmarking 2019*. Fundraising & Philanthropy Australasia Magazine. Retrieved 23 November 2021, from https://www.fpmagazine.com.au/pareto-fundraising-benchmarking-2019-368339/

6. Better Boards. (n.d.). *What is a deductible gift recipient (DGR)?* Retrieved 23 November 2021, from https://betterboards.net/non-profit-fact-sheets/deductible-gift-recipient-dgr/

7. Justice Connect. (2021). The DGR tool. Retrieved 23 November 2021, from https://apps.nfplaw.org.au/dgr/#msdynttrid=yfLsahX6E8ZG25_Ju3kHNgTxYSavUir22ynyFKIXFDQ

8. McLeod, J. (2018, April). The support report: The changing shape of giving and the significant implications for recipients. JB Were. https://aidnetwork.org.au/wp-content/uploads/2019/10/02-JBWere-Support-Report-2018.pdf

9. Pareto Phone. (n.d.). *Pareto benchmarking 2017: Competing priorities*. Retrieved 23 November 2021, from https://paretophone.com/pareto-benchmarking-2017/

10. McLeod, J. (2018, April). *The support report: The changing shape of giving and the significant implications for recipients*. JB Were. https://aidnetwork.org.au/wp-content/uploads/2019/10/02-JBWere-Support-Report-2018.pdf

11. Australian Bureau of Statistics. (2021, September 14). *Residential property price indexes: Eight capital cities*. Retrieved 23 November 2021, from https://www.abs.gov.au/AUSSTATS/abs@.nsf/DetailsPage/6416.0Dec%202019

12. Porter, Michael E. (2004). *Competitive Advantage: Creating and Sustaining Superior Performance*. Free Press. Porter, Michael E. (2008). *On Competition. Harvard Business Review Press*.

13. Philanthropy Australia. (2020). *Giving in Australia: The fast facts*. Retrieved 23 November 2021, from https://www.philanthropy.org.au/tools-resources/fast-facts-and-stats

14. Picco, G. (2020b, June 19). *Canadian charity trends in direct mail*. The Charity Report. Retrieved 23 November 2021, from https://www.thecharityreport.com/news/canadian-charity-trends-in-direct-mail/

15. Ashmore, D., & Grainger, P. (2019). *donorCentrics® Index of direct marketing fundraising 2019: Fourth calendar quarter results*. Blackbaud. https://hello.blackbaud.com/rs/053-MXJ-131/images/Q4-19%20DM%20Index.pdf

16. Ogilvy, D. (1985). *Ogilvy on advertising* (First Edition). Vintage.

17. Andreoni, J., & Payne, A. (2003, June). *Do government grants to private charities crowd out giving or fund-raising?* American Economic Association. Retrieved 23 November 2021, from https://www.aeaweb.org/articles?id=10.1257/000282803322157098

18. Ciconte, B. L. (2003). *Fundraising basics, 2nd edition: A complete guide (Aspen's Fundraising Series for the 21st Century)* (2nd ed.). Jones and Bartlett Publishers, Inc.

19. Sutton-Legaud, P. (n.d.). *Pamela Sutton-Legaud CFRE MBA Senior Consultant - AskRIGHT.* Slide Player. Retrieved 23 November 2021, from https://slideplayer.com/slide/16409801/

20. Durschmied, E. (2013). *The Hinge Factor: How chance and stupidity have changed history.* Hodder & Stoughton.

21. Association of Fundraising Professionals. https://afpglobal.org/; Association for Healthcare Philanthropy. https://www.ahp.org/; Council for Advancement and Support of Education. https://www.case.org/; The Giving Institute. http://www.givinginstitute.org

22. Drucker, P. F. (1990). *Managing the nonprofit organization: Principles and practices* (1st ed.). HarperCollins.